"With insight, wisdom, and e                              Henry answers everything you've wanted to know about prayer but were too embarrassed to ask."

—Debbie Macomber, #1 *New York Times* best-selling author

"If you desire a deeper, focused, effective prayer life, don't miss this book. Janet Holm McHenry's well-researched, biblical exploration of this essential topic will give you an understanding of how to develop a praying lifestyle that fits your God-given personality. Every Christian should read this important book."

—Carol Kent, executive director of Speak Up Ministries, speaker, and author of *He Holds My Hand*

"What does your personality have to do with your prayer life? In *Praying Personalities*, Janet Holm McHenry guides you on a fascinating journey to help you discover your own prayer strengths. She includes personalized tips that will help you deepen the way you talk to God."

—Linda Evans Shepherd, author of *Make Time for Joy*

"Rather than trying to find the *right* way to pray, you can come to God as you are. But how do you do that? *Praying Personalities* will help you discover your natural prayer style, enabling you to draw close to God as you tap into his supernatural power—for your life and for the people you love."

—Joanna Weaver, best-selling author of *Having a Mary Heart in a Martha World* and *Embracing Trust*

"A groundbreaking exploration of the intersection between personality and spirituality, this book encourages readers to learn more about themselves and their unique ways of connecting with God. Whether you're just starting out on your spiritual journey or have been praying for years, Janet's advice will help you connect with God in ways that are true to who *you* are. Her thoughtful analysis of biblical characters and their prayer practices brings a fresh perspective, offering a tailored approach to a more fulfilling spiritual life. If you want to deepen your spiritual journey in a way that's both natural and exciting for your personality, this book is a fantastic resource. I love it!"

—Tricia Goyer, *USA Today* best-selling author of over ninety books, including *Heart Happy*

"Janet has done it again. She's led me into a deeper prayer life through this well-researched book. Not only did I feel more at home with my praying personality, I also gained understanding of how others are created to communicate through prayer."

—Robin Jones Gunn, best-selling author of *Praying for Your Future Husband*

"Prayer is a wonderful opportunity for deeper intimacy with God. However, the mechanics can become ritualistic. With so many formulas and guides sharing specific ways to pray, you may feel prayer is more of a chore than a divine opportunity. In *Praying Personalities*, Janet Holm McHenry helps make prayer an authentic expression to fit every person's unique communication preference. I found this book to be both affirming and challenging as it highlighted my preferred ways to pray and brought to light some prayer routines that did not fit my praying personality. A needed resource to make prayer a natural part of your relationship with God."

—Dr. Saundra Dalton-Smith, best-selling author of *Sacred Rest* and host of *I Choose My Best Life* podcast

"Oh, the freedom to know we can pray in a way that lines up with the unique way God designed each of us! In *Praying Personalities*, author Janet Holm McHenry—a leader in the field of prayer—equips, encourages, and *inspires* the reader to pray in a way that releases the power of prayer and removes much of the common stress, shame, or guilt many Christians feel about being a prayer failure. Yes, read this practical book to gain excitement, meaning, and anticipation in meeting your Creator in prayer!"

—Pam Farrel, author and coauthor of fifty-nine books, including the best-selling *Discovering Wisdom in Proverbs*

"Janet Holm McHenry's *Praying Personalities* meticulously observes how our God-designed personalities directly influence our natural prayer style. We discover that just because our praying style differs from our best friend's doesn't make it wrong or ineffective. McHenry's practical praying applications can help every reader or *pray-er* to enhance their relationship with God by discovering a prayer style that fits who they are by design. This book is a spiritual life changer!"

—Linda Goldfarb, speaker, podcaster, and award-winning co-author of the LINKED® Quick Guide to Personalities series

"This book shares a simple truth about prayer that most never consider. Since much of learning to pray is based upon watching others, it is easy to simply mimic friends' prayer styles but still feel out of sorts in our prayer lives. While learning from others can be helpful, the truth is God has wired each of us to pray the way he intended for us to pray. *Praying Personalities* will help you find that way and will free you to soar in prayer."

—Jonathan Graf, president of Church Prayer Leaders Network

"Books of this depth and insight can only be written by those who have experienced firsthand the truths of which they write and live it out on a daily basis. Janet Holm McHenry's book is an authentic, practical guide on how to pray most effectively, thereby experiencing God's presence daily, renewed and impassioned for his service."

—Jacob George, community pastor and prayer coordinator, Centre Street Church, Calgary, Canada

"For a fresh and liberating approach to overcoming prayer insecurities and guilt, I recommend *Praying Personalities* by Janet Holm McHenry! She uses examples of the prayer styles of biblical figures, personality and spiritual gifts assessments, and learning styles to clarify that prayer is more about building our unique relationship with God and becoming more like Jesus than in following (or not following) rules and methods that others suggest. For a richer praying life, read this book."

—Elaine Helms, SBC national prayer leader, teacher, and award-winning author of *Prayer Without Limits* and *Prayer 101*

"In *Praying Personalities*, Janet Holm McHenry does an incredible job of taking you on a journey of finding your own praying style. She engages the reader with a short, targeted test to actually identify your very own praying personality. The path to enjoyable prayer is truly found in *Praying Personalities*."

—Sylvia Johnson, California state leader for the National Day of Prayer Task Force and intercessory missionary at House of Prayer Sacramento

# *Praying Personalities*

## Finding Your Natural Prayer Style

### JANET HOLM McHENRY

Foreword by Geoff Eckart

KREGEL
PUBLICATIONS

*This book is dedicated with love and respect to
Jennifer Kennedy Dean (1953–2019),
the author whose books on prayer fill most of a shelf in my office.
My friend Jennifer first taught me that rather than having a prayer life,
I should have a praying life, and she helped to inspire my search for a
praying-without-ceasing lifestyle.*

# Contents

# CONTENTS

# Foreword

I READ MORE BOOKS ON prayer than on any other topic, so when I encounter a new one, I look for ways I can apply it to my own prayer life. I found Janet Holm McHenry's book to be unique, fascinating, and a must-read for anyone interested in prayer.

As an amateur musician, I've heard it said that the guitar is the easiest instrument to learn and hardest to master. In some ways that can also be said of prayer. Prayer is both natural and learned. Children can pray from the time they are just beginning to speak. Their prayers seem to flow naturally from their hearts to the heart of the heavenly Father. But prayer is a learning experience, too, as people of all ages can discover new ways to practice it. Prayer is a spiritual journey with the Lord, and like any journey, there is something to learn along the way—no matter how long a person has been praying.

Anyone interested in charting new prayer territories soon realizes that prayer is a challenging discipline. Let's face it—everyone has some level of insecurity when it comes to prayer. For some, that insecurity can lead to guilt and perhaps even shame. As chairman of the National Prayer Committee, I can assure you that prayer insecurity is pervasive. From new believers to those in the highest levels of church and parachurch leadership, the same general theme often surfaces: "When it comes to prayer, I wish I was better." If you feel this way, you are not alone. *Praying Personalities: Finding Your Natural Prayer Style* confronts this insecurity head-on, dispelling the myth that one way or method of praying is better or more effective than another. The reality that you were designed to uniquely commune with God in prayer will set you free from this one-size-fits-all approach.

Janet thoroughly examines the person behind the prayer. She begins with biblical models, citing in detail specific people and passages from the Scriptures that reveal the varied ways they practiced prayer, and weaves those connections into our life experiences. Then she unpacks more modern constructs of personality and integrates them with practical and pragmatic ways to pray. Janet uses her journalistic skill and background to give a generational perspective to prayer and outlines ways to find a distinctive style of prayer.

If you want to pray with more power, expectation, and regularity, read on! This book does something far too few writings on prayer do. It will help you understand how God has uniquely wired you to walk and talk with him.

—REV. GEOFF ECKART,
chairman of the National Prayer Committee
and the National Day of Prayer Task Force

*Chapter 1*

# Debunking Expectations

THE SPEAKER AT THE WOMEN'S conference was mesmerizing. She was inspirational. And she was going to transform my prayer life. All I had to do was buy the $24.99 prayer notebook that would forever organize my prayer lists into seven divided sections—one section for each day of the week. All I had to do was write down the various prayer requests on a checklist sheet, date them, pray, and then wait for God to answer.

It worked something like this. On Mondays I would pray for immediate family. On Tuesdays I would pray for extended family. On Wednesdays I would pray for people in my work circles, on Thursdays for government leaders . . . and so on.

I dove into this new prayer system enthusiastically and followed that routine for about a month. Then life happened—the life I lived as a mom of four kids, a high school English teacher, and a church volunteer. Exhaustion also naturally fell into place as I tried to keep pace with all that was my life. And then guilt followed because I couldn't keep up with the daily praying lists and updates. One morning I found myself asleep face down on the prayer binder.

*Help, Lord. I'm a prayer failure.*

People have all kinds of advice about how, when, and where prayer should be incorporated into a believer's life. They tell others what they do, convinced that their own praying practice is the be-all and end-all for everyone. I even do this, because I get so excited about how my life has changed because of how I pray. However, perhaps a praying lifestyle can come naturally to people in different kinds of ways that mesh best with their unique personalities.

## I Found My Praying Groove

Twenty-three years ago, I started prayerwalking. This practice changed my life—even though it happened rather accidentally. I'd been struggling for several years with my health after my fourth child was born. As a full-time, working mom, I felt I didn't have time to exercise. My evenings were filled with the kids' sports practices and music lessons, as well as volunteer work at our church. I paid for this inactivity, though. I huffed and puffed going up and down stairs in our two-story home. I was overweight. And I needed over-the-counter painkillers to get to sleep at night because my hips and joints hurt.

The worst moment occurred when I stepped out my kitchen door one afternoon and found myself in a crumpled heap because my knee had given way. I knew I needed to do something about my health, but I also knew that God had been nudging me to spend more time with him. As I hobbled back up the steps, I resolved to get up a little earlier the next morning and walk . . . and as I walked, I would pray.

Getting up earlier would not be easy, because I'm not a morning person. However, I'm not an evening person either. I probably have one good hour of the day: lunch—and at that time that "hour" was in actuality a *half* hour in my crazy teaching schedule.

But I did set my alarm for twenty minutes earlier, and when I woke up the next morning, I just threw my sweats over my pajamas and headed out the door. As I started walking, I prayed. At first there was a lot of my-ness in my prayers: my marriage, my kids, my job.

That changed one day when I saw what I call a Single Daddy's Ballet. In the predawn moments as I walked by Toddler Towers on Main Street of my tiny mountain town, I saw a young man in a pickup truck pull up and park diagonally in front of the day care center. Then he jogged around his truck to the other door and swept up a little blanketed bundle, which he passed over to Cheryl, the day care supervisor who had just walked up.

As the young dad, whom I knew to be single, kissed his little girl on her head, she said, "Bye, Daddy. Love you!"

That everyday yet tender scene struck me to the core. *How hard it must be for young moms and dads to leave their little ones in others' care while they head off to work. That young father will drive to Reno, an hour away and then spend more than half his day away from his child.* I immediately started praying for him, for his toddler girl, and for all the workers at the day care.

From that point on, my walking and praying time changed dramatically. Instead of having a my-ness focus for my prayers, I began opening my eyes to my community and praying for the needs that I saw. I now pray for the folks whose businesses I pass. I pray for residents of the homes, for government workers, for commuters, and for teachers, administration, other staff, and students at the local schools.

This simple practice that I began over twenty-five years ago changed me. I lost two dress sizes and those aches and pains. Depression that had clouded most of my adult life disappeared, and paralyzing fears did as well. But prayerwalking also shifted my mindset. Because I prayed for what I saw when I walked, I learned that wherever I am, there's a need for prayer, so my prayerwalking helped me have more of a praying-without-ceasing lifestyle. Instead of having a *prayer* life— pockets of time for prayer—I began to have a *praying* life.

Because the changes in me were so dramatic, I tried to convince others to give prayerwalking a chance. Many have over the years, and many are sold on the practice. However, here's the thing I discovered: a prayerwalking lifestyle works for me, but it may not work for many others. Each of us is different in personality, daily routines, and interests.

I fell into prayerwalking rather circumstantially after years of trying prayer journals and notebooks (I couldn't keep up), scheduled prayer sessions (I fell asleep), and creative prayer drawing (I can't draw). But after years of studying praying people in the Bible, I believe it's possible to find a praying lifestyle that will work for the rest of your life—a natural practice that makes sense with your God-given personality.

So, reader, shed the guilt. Yes, shed that guilt about falling asleep during prayer time or losing track of prayer lists. And let's dig in to learn about various praying lifestyles through a study lens of personality types, spiritual gifts, and those who prayed in the Bible. This book is designed to provide many different tools to help you discover your natural praying lifestyle—not a method to check "prayer" off your day's to-do list, but a practice that will keep you in step with the God who loves you all day long.

If, as you read the chapters, you're itching to uncover your praying personality, just take the Praying Personality Quiz at the end of this book. (You can use the QR code to use the online option or take the written quiz at the end of the book.) You may find it gives you a reference point as you read the remaining chapters.

## What's Personality Got to Do with It?

My personality has a lot to do with the fact that prayerwalking works for me. I can't sit still and I'm impatient and unable to relax well. When we go on a vacation to the beach, while I *say* I want to sit in a chair by the water and read books, in actuality I cannot do that for more than an hour, if even that. I am a driven do-er.

I also love having a problem to solve. I don't love the problem, but I love the challenge of finding a solution to it. I am a confident and motivated committee of one. In fact, if I am in a committee, I'm often the chairperson and just as often the one doing most of the work. Call me a control freak. That's an ugly truth with which I struggle a lot.

These are some of the traits of what is known as the choleric temperament. My strengths include that I am ambitious, passionate, leader-like, and goal-oriented. However, my weak characteristics are often my downfall: I am also impatient, argumentative, intolerant, and short-tempered. In other words, I constantly must be aware of my weaknesses so that I temper them, because often I can alienate others in my push to get things done.

In my young adulthood I studied the classic temperaments in several books published by the Christian book publishing industry. Those authors went back to the works of Hippocrates (460–370 BC), who defined four temperaments:

- Sanguine: the social, life-of-the party personality
- Choleric: the ruling, dominant type
- Melancholy: the meticulous analyzer
- Phlegmatic: the relaxed, content stabilizer

While these temperaments may seem to put people in boxes, it's typical for people to find they have characteristics of more than one. Each one has strengths to offer the world; each one has attendant weaknesses. The purpose behind studying personality types, then, is not to simply categorize yourself or others, but to understand yourself, see your strengths, recognize your weaknesses, and then live up to your Christlike potential. The personality studies can also help you connect with a certain praying style. Later in this book I'll explain the temperaments in more depth, and you might see yourself in one or more of them.

Another way to understand yourself is through more modern personality studies such as the Myers-Briggs Type Indicator. You may have taken that assessment, which leads to a label such as ISTJ or ENTP. When introduced to that personality assessment years ago, I struggled with the label and could never keep straight what those letters meant. Also, each time I took one of those tests over the last couple of decades, I got a different result. I don't like being put into what seems like a psychologist's matrix with a predictable behavior and outcome and textbook solutions to my issues. The sixteen variations of that assessment are often laid out in a grid—seemingly affirming my impression of being stuck in a pigeonhole.

However, when I recently studied Myers-Briggs again, I discovered the assessment boils down to four questions:

- Are you outwardly or inwardly focused?
- How do you best take in information?
- How do you make decisions?
- How do you prefer living your outer life?

Instead of doing the quiz, I thought about and answered those questions. I found I am more inwardly focused (I); I prefer sensory, concrete details (S) to generalized concepts; I make decisions based on logical thinking (T) rather than my feelings; and I judge (J) by rules and prefer concrete plans, rather than live spontaneously. In discussing any of the personality assessments in this book, we'll take this same approach and look at root questions that underlie the theories.

Knowing all this helps me be aware of the reasons I pray the way I do. Here's an example. I just put out a prayer plea to a couple of close friends in a text. One of those friends told me I should just start play-ing worship music and sing along. However, while that might work for this friend who listens to worship music whenever she can, it doesn't work for me. I prefer quiet, so I can hear God's still voice directing my next steps. That's just one way personality can play out in a praying lifestyle, and we'll examine other personality sorters as well.

You will find that many different forms of personality assessment are included in this book—from those Greek temperaments to modern assessments based on psychology to the Enneagram. (Please note my inclusion of these does not mean I endorse any of them, other than the LINKED® Quick Guide to Personalities by Linda Gilden and Linda Goldfarb.[1]) I include a variety because not all of us click with each one. Some assessments make complete sense to some of us, while others appear to be fuzzy gibberish. Plus, different seasons of life reveal additional insights, so if you took a personality test many years ago, you'll find you understand yourself better now—thus a newer personality test will be more accurate.

With each test, I examined the underlying questions that distinguish one personality from another, because often multiple-choice tests just don't bring about a true result. As you read about each personality, I encourage you to think about those questions and how you'd answer them. Those will be helpful indicators of your personality that will help you find your natural praying style. And I encourage you to take the Praying Personality Quiz at the end of the book and read through all the personality chapters in this book, so you can glean additional bits of understanding about yourself.

## What Do Spiritual Gifts Have to Do with It?

When Craig and I were both twenty-nine, we had finally finished college and his service years in the army. We were ready to settle down, build a house, raise kiddos, and plug in to a local church. Opportunities to serve in our small-town church were endless: music ministry, Sunday school for kids and adults, visitation of seniors, junior church, church board leadership, and more.

I jumped in with both feet and soon found myself overwhelmed with the number of responsibilities I had taken on. In fact, one Easter morning I sang in the community sunrise service, helped prepare the multichurch breakfast, sang with the choir during the regular service, taught junior church, fixed a big midday meal at home, and then collapsed that afternoon a bit peeved that others hadn't helped. The problem was I did not have an awareness of my spiritual gifts and a sense of calling on my life.

Three passages in Scripture (found in Rom. 12, 1 Cor. 12, and Eph. 4) provide lists of spiritual gifts, which are prophecy, teaching, apostleship, evangelism, shepherding, helping, wisdom, knowledge, faith, healing, miracles, discernment, tongues, interpretation of tongues, service, exhortation, giving, leadership, and mercy. Questions that help us decide what spiritual gifts we may have include the following:

- Why do you do what you do?
- What motivates you?
- Do you do what you do because of love?
- Do you want to strengthen others?
- Are you more word-oriented or deed-oriented?

Do you see how these questions come back again to the idea of personality—the person God has made us to be? While it's not healthy to obsess about ourselves and our personality continually, understanding how God designed us is helpful in guiding us to a natural prayer style. Let me explain.

Earlier I mentioned that I had taken on way too many roles in our church. I simply wanted to help. I saw needs and thought, *I could do that!* Well, sure, I could, but God had also designed me to be a wife, mother, and teacher—and if I threw myself into too many other roles, I would be exhausted. That exhaustion filtered into my spiritual disciplines as well. I didn't have time for prayer when I was running from one thing to another and hadn't taken a step back to get a bigger picture of my life and callings.

A spiritual gifts test I took showed that my greatest gift is hospitality, which I exercise in hosting prayer groups. Another gift is administration, which I put into practice through the prayer coordinator position at my church. I draw on discernment as I'm prayerwalking and asking God to reveal the needs of the people in the homes and businesses I pass. Sometimes I'll just know a need and pray: that's the spiritual gift of knowledge. Later someone will tell me a situation that has come to pass, and I'll say, "Wow, I prayed for that." And clearly, you know I *exercise* prayer for my community. Knowing our spiritual gifts will give us insight as to how they can influence our praying style.

## What Do Biblical People Have to Do with It?

I was not born in Missouri, but I am a "show me" kind of girl. When I first started prayerwalking, I began reading the Bible from cover to cover, over and over again, to learn more about prayer—essentially for God to show me what it is. Whenever I saw a prayer or a related reference, I wrote a circled *P* in the margin. I also read, marked up, and reread a book called *All the Prayers of the Bible* by Herbert Lockyer.[2] I wanted to observe the personal prayer practices of characters in the Bible and how they prayed. I wanted to see how they addressed God and talked with him. And I began to notice how some argued with God, some complained, some spent time in worship, and some simply listened and obeyed God's instructions without a word in response.

I also saw that biblical characters' prayer practices seemingly lined up with other behaviors that would indicate a certain personality or temperament type. Here's one example. Paul demonstrated organized thinking in his letters; he started with prayer and ended with prayer. We also know he was goal-minded and exhorted his readers to "pray without ceasing" (1 Thess. 5:17 NKJV). We get the impression that this on-the-run pray-er was himself constantly in prayer. So he might have had a choleric temperament—one who was driven to be a mover and shaker in prayer for the sake of the kingdom.

As I began to make these sorts of connections in the Bible, I came to understand there is not one prayer practice that is better than another.

Different people in the Bible prayed in different manners that seemingly reflected the kind of person they were. The same would be true for you and me. Because we often identify with different characters in the Bible, we'll start in part one by examining those praying personalities in the Bible.

The more I've read the Bible, the more I understand that Bible heroes and heroines were just people like you and me. They had strengths, and they had weak spots. Those characteristics played out in their lives because of their God-given personalities and their own personal choices— good and bad.

As you learn more about yourself through the study of God's Word and the various personality types, it is my hope you will resonate with one or more of these biblical people and find a praying lifestyle that deepens your relationship with the Lord, leading you to your own praying-without-ceasing mindset.

So as you read *Praying Personalities*, consider these questions for the three sections of the book:

- Biblical praying styles: Which Bible characters do you resonate with, and why? What one or more of their prayer practices make the best sense for you?
- Personality types: How has God made you? What praying styles seem to connect with you?
- Spiritual gifts: What are your gifts, and how could they connect naturally to a praying practice?

At the end of each discussion of either a biblical praying style, personality type, or spiritual gift, you will find a feature called Prayer Pointers. These will provide suggestions that are natural praying practices for that kind of personality.

Understanding who you are in Christ will help you shed false expectations and guilt about what others say your prayer life should be or even some false ideal you have created in your own mind. Instead, you can just pray—and find freedom as you meet God with the very best offering: yourself.

──────── DISCUSSION QUESTIONS ────────

1. What was it that intrigued you about reading this book?
2. What kinds of expectations do you have about how prayer should happen?
3. Who is someone you admire for his or her prayer life? How does that person pray?
4. What do you think about personality assessments? Is there a personality type that resonates with you? If so, which one and why?
5. What biblical praying person do you admire for his or her prayer(s) or praying style and why?
6. Do you have a regular praying practice that works for you? Explain your answer.

# PART ONE

## Biblical Praying Styles

*Chapter 2*

# Cerebral Pray-ers

MORE THAN TWENTY YEARS AGO when I started prayerwalking, I began noticing ways that God answered my prayers. Oddly enough, some of those I found right in the *Sierra Booster*, our little town's tabloid newspaper that comes out every two weeks (the editor uses the term *fortnightly*)—without headlines over news stories (because they take up too much room, I've been told). One issue invited the whole town to a couple's wedding just weeks after God nudged me to pray they would get married. Another issue displayed photos of a young woman from our town carrying the Olympic torch just months after she'd been diagnosed with multiple sclerosis—a woman I'd been praying for as I passed the office where she worked. The stories of answered prayers go on and on.

Encouraged, I was also confused. How could my prayers have effect? Why were these prayers answered and not others? What *was* prayer, anyway? Those questions and more created a hunger inside of me to learn more about prayer, so I began reading the Bible each year from cover to cover on a prayer quest of sorts, underlining and noting passages where people in the Bible prayed, how God responded, as well as specific teachings on prayer. I've done that now for more than twenty years and have identified many praying styles among biblical people.

This part of the book will examine some of those praying people in the Bible. What I have found is they can be identified in four different ways that relate to their personalities. First, some of us operate more from a mental or cerebral framework. We approach life, the faith, and even God in our prayer life more analytically. Then others of us are more emotionally wired. We process and react to life through our feelings and pray emotively. A third personality grouping for pray-ers includes an instinctively spiritual or devotional filter through which some of us see life and approach a praying style. Lastly, others of us are robust and physical in how we traverse life, and such a tendency could influence our prayer practices.

This chapter and the next three will examine each of these biblical praying personalities:

- The Cerebral Pray-ers
- The Emotive Pray-ers
- The Devotional Pray-ers
- The Physical Pray-ers

The design behind starting with biblical characters is twofold. First, a biblical framework always provides the best starting point for us in a study about prayer. After all, God started the conversation with humankind's first people, Adam and Eve, and we can learn more about God's design for prayer as we look at various biblical people's lives.

And second, you might see yourself in one or more of those characters, who could help you breathe a sigh of relief: *Maybe I am doing this right!* The study of the biblical characters will help you see that your praying lifestyle can naturally arise out of how God has made you.

This chapter will focus on six biblical characters. First, let's look at Adam.

## The Questioner: Adam

Adam is unique as the only person God created from no other human being but from the dust of the ground, with God breathing life into him (Gen. 2:7). This first human form, Genesis 1:27 tells us, God created in his own image. As the first two humans, Adam and Eve, who was created from Adam's rib, had the privilege of the Lord God's sole attention—their own prayer closet of sorts being the garden of Eden. God could have created Adam and Eve and then left the planet without any instructions, but instead, he chose to give them some. Those instructions, found in Genesis 1:28–30, begin the conversation between God and humans that we call prayer:

> God blessed them and said to them, "Be fruitful and increase in number; fill the earth and subdue it. Rule over the fish in the sea and the birds in the sky and over every living creature that moves on the ground."
>
> Then God said, "I give you every seed-bearing plant on the face of the whole earth and every tree that has fruit with seed in it. They will be yours for food. And to all the beasts of the earth and all the birds in the sky and all the creatures that move along the ground—everything that has the breath of life in it—I give every green plant for food." And it was so.

God began the conversation with man, and Scripture tells us "it was very good" after he created man on that sixth day of creation (Gen. 1:31). After the earlier days of creation, God had said "it was good" five times. After man was created, it was *very good*, in God's view. And then man messed up the conversation.

God gave Adam just a few instructions: (1) be fruitful and increase in number, (2) subdue the earth, (3) rule over other living creatures, and (4) eat from any tree in the garden except the tree of the knowledge of good and evil (Gen. 1:28–30; 2:16–17). When we raised our kids, Craig and I gave them instructions every day. "Come home right after school." "Don't forget to feed the dog." "No, you can't have any friends over unless I am home." The assumed response was always, "Okay." Perhaps Adam just nodded, but I think it's fair to assume that he and Eve said, "Yes, God. We understand."

And yet Adam and Eve disobeyed God. They ate from the tree of the knowledge of good and evil. They questioned God's parenting style and tried to put themselves in a position equal with their Creator. Those of us who've parented children know that disobedience in particular and sin in general put strain on our conversations. When mutual respect is broken, relationships suffer.

Let's look at how Adam responded when God confronted him. When God asked Adam where he was, Adam said, "I heard you in the garden, and I was afraid because I was naked; so I hid" (Gen. 3:10). When God asked him how he knew he was naked and if he had eaten of the tree of knowledge, Adam said, "The woman you put here with me—she gave me some fruit from the tree, and I ate it" (Gen. 3:12). These were the last words we hear from Adam, a man who chose to disobey God, who tried to hide from him, and who blamed his wife for his sins. The tone of his responses to God demonstrates Adam's shame, yet also his questioning and defensive posture as he tried to explain himself. The picture of the garden as an intimate setting for prayerful conversation with the Creator was broken.

But while there were consequences for Adam and Eve's choices to distance themselves from God, their Creator did not abandon the relationship. He clothed them (Gen. 3:21), blessed them with children (Gen. 4:1–2, 25), and continued to converse with their children as we see in Genesis 4. In other words, God was still near to them and responded to their needs and choices.

While Adam was seemingly a negative example of a praying person, what we can take away from his prayerful interaction with God is that if we have a questioning personality that filters into our prayers, it's all right to have hard conversations with God. We can ask questions of him. We can get defensive and resistant. We can mess up and still go to him. Our questions can draw us closer to our Creator, who started the conversation with his creation. And he can withstand our questioning posture because, like loving parents, he does not wash his hands of us.

Prayer is all about relationship. This may be hard for the Questioner who, like an attorney, is trained to think of all the problems of a matter rather than wait for God's direction. As we pray over the many seasons of our lives—with a compliant perspective or not—we ultimately become more like the One who seeks us out, whether we are hiding or not. So if you are a Questioner—if you see problems without answers—you are going to the right place when you pray.

## The Thinker: Job

While Adam had everything given to him in the garden of Eden, Job had just about everything taken away. In a heavenly brokerage that would prove Job's faithfulness, God allowed Satan to bring about the loss of his ten children, his livestock, and his servants. Job's response to these first losses was worship:

> Naked I came from my mother's womb,
>  and naked I will depart.
> The LORD gave and the LORD has taken away;
>  may the name of the LORD be praised.
> (Job 1:21)

Then when God allowed Satan to afflict Job with painful sores from head to foot, Job told his bitter wife, "Shall we accept good from God, and not trouble?" (Job 2:10). Job's faithfulness to God helped him see God's sovereign faithfulness to him over his lifetime—and we see his reasoning skills played out prayerfully throughout the rest of the book of Job. Here are a few examples:

Why did I not perish at birth,
and die as I came from the womb?
(Job 3:11)

Remember, O God, that my life is but a breath;
My eyes will never see happiness again.
(Job 7:7)

But how can mere mortals prove their innocence before God?
(Job 9:2)

To God belong wisdom and power;
Counsel and understanding are his. . . .
To him belong strength and insight;
both deceived and deceiver are his.
(Job 12:13, 16)

A person's days are determined;
you have decreed the number of his months
and have set limits he cannot exceed.
(Job 14:5)

As Job processed the arguments with his less-than-helpful friends—Eliphaz, Bildad, Zophar, and later the younger Elihu—we see Job wanted to understand his suffering, express his doubts, think through God's design for his life and humanity's in general, and ultimately respond faithfully to the Lord. Over and over Job questioned God as his friends offered limited if not incorrect theological responses, and then

God revealed a long discourse about his power as revealed through creation. To this Job replied reverently:

> I know that you can do all things;
>> no purpose of yours can be thwarted.
>
> You asked, "Who is this that obscures my plans without knowledge?"
>> Surely I spoke of things I did not understand,
>> things too wonderful for me to know.
>
> You said, "Listen now, and I will speak;
>> I will question you,
>> and you shall answer me."
> My ears had heard of you
>> but now my eyes have seen you.
> Therefore I despise myself
>> and repent in dust and ashes.
>
> (Job 42:2–6)

Job was a thinker. He used his reasoning skills to appeal to God in prayer—again, like an attorney, but in a more prosecutorial style. Job was not merely thinking aloud; he was praying, and his prayers turned his face toward God in his answer-seeking. That kind of prayer is okay too.

God gave us brains to reason, to solve problems, to understand. As human beings we look for direction for our lives, and we seek understanding for the pain we experience. We use our brains to reason with God too. We want to know the *why* behind our frustrations and suffering. That may seem to be a resistant and unbiblical response to God's sovereign plan for our lives, but even Jesus prayed, "My God, my God, why have you forsaken me?" (Matt. 27:46). Thinking, reasoning, and appealing to God in prayer are just the right responses, actually. We go to the Problem Solver when we are in crisis or when we simply are confused and need direction.

If, like me, you appreciate arguments that are logical in nature as opposed to emotional, you can take that to your prayer posture. Another way to look at this is to think of how your pastor might deliver a sermon. Some pastors tell engaging, funny, or even emotional stories that help sway their pew-sitters' opinions. On the other hand, some simply appeal to a sense of logic through a rational discourse of God's Word and what it says. While I love a good story, I prefer that an argument come down to the truth about who God is and what he has said in his Word. *Just the facts, ma'am.* If that sounds like you, God invites you into his heavenly courtroom, where you can present your case—which is always welcome—and listen to his reasoning—which is always right.

## The Dialoguer: Moses

Have you ever felt you were in a two-way dialogue with the Lord? We see that kind of exchange frequently when we look at the life of Moses. It all starts over two chapters at the beginning of Exodus (chaps. 3–4) in a back-and-forth conversation, the Lord abruptly calling Moses to lead the Hebrews out of Egypt and Moses responding with numerous objections. Here are paraphrased bits and pieces of that interaction:

God: Go to Pharoah to bring my people out of Egypt.
Moses: Who am I to try such a thing?
God: I will be with you and you will worship me.
Moses: But who should I say sent me?
God: You tell them I sent you. Get the leaders together.
Moses: What if they won't listen to me?

Then the Lord performed two miracles to prove his miracle-making ability: turning a staff into a snake then back into a staff and turning Moses's hand leprous and then normal again.

God: Try doing that so they believe you.
Moses: But God, I am a lousy public speaker.
God: I made your mouth. I will put the right words in it.
Moses: Please send someone else.
God: Your brother, Aaron, will be your mouthpiece. The miracles will help too.

The conversation reminds me of my high school English students when they tried to get out of doing presentations in class: they often took more minutes and used more words arguing with me than they would have spent in front of the class. How Moses thought he could talk God out of sending him on such a mission is curious, but as Moses was raised in Pharoah's home, he had insider information, and his language skills and understanding of the king of Egypt would have proved valuable. This early exchange in Moses's relationship with the Lord set a stage for later prayerful encounters:

- Moses's complaint about being sent to Pharoah, who made work conditions even harder for the Hebrews (Exod. 5:22–6:8)
- A dialogue reiterating God's instruction to have Aaron help Moses (Exod. 6:28–7:7)
- A desperate cry for water and God's response (Exod. 17:4–7)
- The Mount Sinai encounter: covenant, instructions, Ten Commandments (Exod. 19–31)

It's interesting to watch Moses become a more confident advocate in prayer for the sake of the people as the story unfolds. Instead of worrying about his own limits and safety, he developed into a man who understood his role as the intermediary between the Israelites and the Lord God. This played out when the people talked Aaron into building a golden calf to worship. Moses sought mercy from the Lord, whose anger was leading toward destroying the people (Exod. 32:7–10).

Moses, who'd earlier said he wasn't a good speaker, presented a power-ful argument for saving the people, and the Lord relented (vv. 11–14). Moses's frequent dialogues with the Lord developed his character into a man who stopped worrying about himself and instead saw the larger picture for saving the Hebrew nation and his own calling to deliver the people into the promised land of Canaan.

Perhaps you see yourself as a Dialoguer if you tend to talk to God all day long. That kind of praying-without-ceasing lifestyle evolves as we see that the day's tasks before us are reasons for prayer—for dia-logue with our heavenly Father. Struggles and complaints are reasons to pray. Blessings and provision are reasons to pray. Simple, autopilot, daily tasks are reasons to pray. Those with whom we live and work and encounter are reasons to pray. And as we go more frequently to God for those reasons, prayer becomes more natural throughout our day . . . a stream of consciousness dialogue for whatever is before us.

## The Sign Requester: Gideon

God raised up Gideon as a judge for Israel when the Israelites fell into sin and suffered from seven years of Midianite oppression. However, as the weakest in his family, which was the weakest in the tribe of Manasseh, Gideon had doubts. In a prayerful exchange he asked the Lord to prove himself: Gideon wanted a sign that he was actually hear-ing from the Lord God: "If now I have found favor in your eyes, give me a sign that it is really you talking to me. Please do not go away until I come back and bring my offering and set it before you" (Judg. 6:17–18). That offering the Lord consumed with fire, convincing Gideon that he was conversing with the true God. Gideon then built an altar to the Lord (called The Lord is Peace) and tore down his own father's altar to Baal, causing a violent reaction from a local crowd that joined forces with other armies to challenge Gideon.

Gideon continued to pray for signs from God because he needed more convincing for what was ahead.

If you will save Israel by my hand as you have promised—look, I will place a wool fleece on the threshing floor. If there is dew only on the fleece and all the ground is dry, then I will know that you will save Israel by my hand, as you said. (Judg. 6:36–37)

The Lord accepted the challenge, and the fleece alone was wet the next morning. But Gideon needed yet another assurance and asked for a final sign: to make the fleece dry overnight with dry ground around it. And God provided yet another sign for Gideon.

While continually asking God for signs can be a faithless prayer pattern, God did honor Gideon's requests, as he may indeed honor ours.

*Lord, if I am meant to take this job, provide more salary than my last job.*

*God, if you want me to get married, bring the right person into my life soon.*

*I need a new car, Lord, but I want a blue one. Let me find a blue one at this lot.*

Sign Requesters need intellectual certainty. They can't make decisions without understanding the situation and the ramifications for various choices. Those who continually ask God for signs may be in an early stage of their faith. But this becomes problematic long term because faith strength only comes from trusting God for the outcome.

We see from Gideon's story that God did honor his requests, but we also see how God put Gideon to the test—shrinking his army from thirty-two thousand to three hundred to face the dreaded Midianite army. Gideon prayed for signs, which God provided; but God then tested Gideon's faith.

Sign Requesters need to know God is real, but the stories of biblical characters and God's faithfulness to them provide a foundation for praying in faith, rather than from a framework of continual doubt. He may bless Sign Requesters with those signs but ultimately faith requires tests of us too.

## The Problem Solvers: Elijah and Hezekiah

I've sometimes called myself a foul-weather friend, because while I may seem distant in uneventful times, I'm at the front porch knocking with a warm dinner when a friend is sick or is grieving. In fact, I just delivered one today for a friend down with COVID. We do not see some biblical characters praying until they are in crisis mode or see a critical need for someone else. Such is true as we read the accounts of Elijah and Hezekiah.

Elijah was a prophet during the reign of the seventh king of the northern kingdom, Israel, who was the husband of Jezebel. Ahab and Jezebel were evil, and as a prophet, Elijah never had good news for the pair. His prayers were focused on problem-solving in response to crises. The New Testament writer James used Elijah as an example of a righteous man whose prayers were powerful and effective:

> Elijah was a human being, even as we are. He prayed earnestly that it would not rain, and it did not rain on the land for three and a half years. Again he prayed, and the heavens gave rain, and the earth produced its crops. (James 5:17–18)

The people of Israel were worshipping Baal, a god of fertility and lord of the rain clouds. The Lord's answers to Elijah's prayers showed the people worshipping that worthless god that the Lord God was not only lord over creation but also the one who would convey judgment for their apostasy.

Elijah's other prayer examples show how he turned to prayer in problem-solving mode:

- Raising the widow of Zarephath's son (1 Kings 17:19–24)
- Proving the Lord was God in Israel to the 450 prophets of Baal by calling on God to bring fire out of a watered-down pile of wood (1 Kings 18:36–39)

- Bringing about rain from clear skies as a warning for Ahab (1 Kings 18:41–46)
- Appealing to God for release from life (1 Kings 19:3–9) and becoming strengthened instead
- Appealing to God for his defense and hearing God in a gentle whisper (1 Kings 19:9–13)

Certainly, as the Lord's prophet during a very difficult regime under cruel Ahab, Elijah kept close to the Lord for his very life as well as the directives and prophecies God wanted him to speak to Ahab and Israel. His difficult calling to be God's spokesman on earth was exhausting—requiring prayerful responses to one crisis after another.

As the prayer coordinator for my church in Reno, one of the most frequent requests I receive to pass along to others is one asking for God's direction. Every day people want to know how God would guide them. So it makes sense that those in power who trust in God would also ask for the Lord's guidance. Just under a hundred years after Elijah, in the southern kingdom of Judah, Hezekiah became king, with Scripture's notation, "He held fast to the LORD and did not stop following him" (2 Kings 18:6). When we hold fast to the Lord, we rely on him for everything, especially those situations of great challenge.

Hezekiah's challenge was the impending attack of the Assyrian king, Sennacherib, a threat that sent the king of Judah into sackcloth mourning and temple prayer. Hezekiah's response to the Assyrian king's letter mocking the Lord God was prayer: "Now, LORD our God, deliver us from his hand, so that all the kingdoms of the earth may know that you alone, LORD, are God" (2 Kings 19:19). And God's response? The angel of the Lord put to death 185,000 men in the night. God honored Hezekiah's sincere crisis prayer.

But Hezekiah also prayed for himself when he was facing impending death due to illness: "Remember, LORD, how I have walked before you faithfully and with wholehearted devotion and have done what is good in your eyes" (2 Kings 20:3). The Lord not only delivered Hezekiah from the Assyrian king and his forces, but also delivered Hezekiah from death—adding another fifteen years to his life. So we see how God heard the prayers of righteous kings, not just righteous prophets.

What personality runs to prayer when problems prompt him or her? Well, all of us, right? But there's a special sensitivity in those who see others' pain and instinctively go to the Problem Solver on their knees. They may physically hurt because others hurt; they live out the "carry each another's burdens" admonition (Gal. 6:2). They themselves are natural-born problem solvers but have learned that prayer is the best problem-solving strategy. Problem Solvers do not panic in dire times but instead instinctively go to prayer.

Here's a sticky set of questions, though. What about our heartfelt prayers that go unanswered? What about our loved ones whose lives are not extended extra years? What about those times when we ask God to remove figurative warring enemies from our lives . . . and he doesn't? What if we are living a clean life but only hear silence to our sincere requests?

Problem Solvers have learned that as they go to God in prayer, they are moving into his zone. They understand that the purpose of prayer is less about answers but more about access to the living God, and as they spend more time in prayer—in crisis or not—they take on more of his likeness and understand more of his nature. And his nature is good and worthy of their trust. They know he will see them through whatever is ahead. Prayer itself is an initial indicator of faith; that we go to God at all indicates our first steps of belief.

Cerebral Pray-ers may not be quick leapers; they need to understand the trustworthiness of the Lord and his plan. They want to test the faith waters a bit, ask for signs, and even offer a bit of debate in the prayer throne room. Because God made different personalities, he can confirm that he is real to those who need such confirmation. However, that assurance may also come in the form of God's Word, the counsel of other believers, or even circumstances. Eventually, the Doubting Thomases among us will demonstrate growing faith in the Heavenly One we approach in prayer.

──────── PRAYER POINTERS ────────

- Go to God with your questions.
- Be figuratively naked in your confessions.
- Feel free to explain yourself, talking through your understanding of a situation with the Lord.
- Ask God for signs as you face decision-making situations.
- Pray for understanding of hard circumstances, then prayerfully give your situations over to him.
- Begin to seek him first with your questions *before* you take action, and wait for his response.
- Pray for guidance for big-picture decisions and trust him to guide you in the resulting details.
- Accept that God's thoughts are not your thoughts. What may seem logical to you may not be what God has purposed.

──────── DISCUSSION QUESTIONS ────────

1. What do your prayers sound like? Are they simple and to the point? Are they longer with a rationale for your request or more emotionally charged? Or are they presented in a different way?
2. Adam got defensive with and questioned God. Job utilized attorney-like reasoning skills in his prayers. What do you think of their approach of the Lord?
3. Moses tried to talk his way out of God's call on his life to lead the people from slavery back to the Promised Land. How do you feel about that prayerful approach?

4. Some people like Gideon need signs from God. Recall a time when you asked God for a sign that would help you make a decision.
5. For what circumstances did Elijah and Hezekiah approach God in prayer?
6. What Prayer Pointers at the end of the chapter make sense to you?

*Chapter 3*

# Emotive Pray-ers

IN ONE OF MY RESPONSIBILITIES on the California leadership team for the National Day of Prayer, I meet weekly for an hour or more on a prayer call with others on the team. It's interesting to hear others pray. While I tend to be succinct and to the point, others pour out heart-stirred words accompanied by tears and even sobs. These folks are what I would call Emotive Pray-ers. We all have emotions that can influence how we speak and even pray, but Emotive Pray-ers carry others' and their own burdens emotionally into the throne room of prayer. This chapter will look at three Emotive Pray-ers from the Bible: Hannah, David, and Jeremiah.

## The Emotion-Driven Pray-er: Hannah

I get prayer requests all day long from family, friends, church folks, intercessor leaders of the California National Day of Prayer organization, and others with whom I'm connected on social media—and I pray as soon as I receive them and send them out as requested. I've led many prayer ministries over the years and have seen God answer time and time again. But sometimes I find myself flat on the couch. The prayer burdens can be heavy, and it's not infrequent that I find myself emotionally exhausted. In Hannah we see such a sea of emotions that inspire her prayers.

When it's the heart's desire of a woman to have a child, and she cannot, her prayers can be full of angst. I have friends who live with such struggles—and a couple of them have even written books on the subject. Here is Hannah's prayerful vow:

> LORD Almighty, if you will only look upon your servant's misery and remember me, and not forget your servant but give her a son, then I will give him to the LORD for all the days of his life, and no razor will ever be used on his head. (1 Sam. 1:11)

Hannah was so overcome with emotion that the priest Eli thought she was drunk. "No," she told him: she was "deeply troubled" and simply pouring out her soul to the Lord out of her anguish and grief (vv. 15–16). That's emotive prayer—a cry to the Lord out of pain. And where better to go when we are in such deep depths of despair but to the source of consolation, Jehovah-Jireh? This name means "it shall be seen" or "it shall be provided"—a name for the Lord that arose out of Abraham's sacrificial willingness to give up his own son.

As the Lord provided a sacrifice for Abraham, he also provided a son for Hannah and her husband, Elkanah. As she promised, Hannah dedicated Samuel to the Lord's service, saying to the priest, Eli, "'I prayed for this child, and the LORD has granted me what I asked of him. So now I give him to the LORD. For his whole life he will be given over to the LORD.' And he worshiped the LORD there" (vv. 27–28). Then Hannah prayed again out of the joy of her heart—a ten-verse prayer, which starts

> My heart rejoices in the LORD;
> in the LORD my horn is lifted high.
> My mouth boasts over my enemies,
> for I delight in your deliverance.

> There is no one holy like the LORD;
>   there is no one besides you;
>   there is no Rock like our God.
>                    (1 Sam. 2:1–2)

From disconsolate sorrow to delightful joy, Hannah's prayers swing, giving us the freedom to pray out of the heights and depths of our emotions. Some of us are simply more emotional people in personality, and our praying style will reflect that makeup. As I mentioned earlier, my own prayers typically are more matter-of-fact in nature, but when a matter of injustice or pain arises, I, too, pray passionately with a natural overflow of heightened voice and perhaps even tears.

And since the Lord has created us—complete with our emotional makeup—and since Jesus himself wept over Lazarus (John 11:35) and Jerusalem (Luke 19:41), we see God does not discount emotive prayer as less sophisticated or worthy than prayer that originates out of our intellect or reasoning. The Lord hears and answers all kinds of prayers and loves all those who come to him.

## The Poet: David

I have a friend, Sam, who literally prays in poetry. We meet each Saturday morning for up to two hours through that conference call with other leaders of the National Day of Prayer organization in California. When Sam hears a prayer need that someone shares, he often responds with a poem he has written right there on the spot. Heartfelt and moving, it stirs our hearts in such a way that simple prose might not. David was such a pray-er.

While David wrote seventy-five of the Psalms, surprisingly there are only a handful of his prayers mentioned in the biography of his life, as recorded in 1 Samuel 16 through 1 Kings 2:10. In the prayers mentioned throughout his life's story, we see a pattern of his "inquiring" of the Lord about timing for battle attacks, with the Lord responding "Go." The content of his psalms, though, differs.

We find David's poetic praying life in the Psalms. He prayed in lyrics and worshipped in songs of many types. In fact, we see that David's prayers are found in all the different types that scholars use to categorize the psalms:[1]

*Wisdom psalms*, such as Psalm 133:

> How good and pleasant it is
> when God's people live together in unity!
> (v. 1)

*Royal (kingship) psalms*, such as Psalm 2, also a *messianic psalm* that foretells Jesus as Messiah:

> Why do the nations conspire
> and the peoples plot in vain?
> The kings of the earth rise up
> and the rulers band together
> against the LORD and against his anointed.
> (vv. 1–2)

*Penitential psalms*, such as Psalm 51:

> Cleanse me with hyssop, and I will be clean;
> wash me, and I will be whiter than snow. . . .
> My sacrifice, O God, is a broken spirit;
> a broken and contrite heart
> you, God, will not despise.
> (vv. 7, 17)

*Songs of confidence*, such as Psalm 23:

> The LORD is my shepherd; I lack nothing.
>     He makes me lie down in green pastures,
> he leads me beside quiet waters,
>     he refreshes my soul.
>
> (vv. 1–3)

*Laments*, such as Psalm 139 (David wrote thirty-one of the thirty-nine laments in the Psalms):

> Where can I go from your Spirit?
>     Where can I flee from your presence?
> If I go up to the heavens, you are there;
>     If I make my bed in the depths, you are there.
>
> (vv. 7–8)

*Thanksgiving and praise hymns*, such as Psalm 40:

> He put a new song in my mouth,
>     a hymn of praise to our God.
> Many will see and fear the LORD
>     and put their trust in him.
>
> (v. 3)

In other words, David wrote out his prayers lyrically to reflect various moods and heart-inspired ideas.

What kind of personality breaks out in poetry as a form of prayer? An introspective creative. A musical individual who understands rhythm and can see word pictures. A sensitive person who instinctively reflects on life, people, and situations. Someone who appreciates alone, quiet times. We know David danced and sang to express his worship. While his wife Michal disapproved of his doing so in public, to David it was a natural expression.

Such may be true for you too. I have praying friends who play worship music during their Bible study and prayer times . . . and some throughout the entire day. If that describes you, you may be an Emotive Pray-er. You pray with all your "feels" and sing or hum to music continually—connecting your heart to God's.

## The Lamenter: Jeremiah

Do you break out in tears often when you pray? I do sometimes. The tears may be from a heart connection to someone in pain, a feeling of my own remorse, or even a burden for the spiritually lost. Jeremiah has been called the "weeping prophet" because his prayers lamented the people's disregard for God in Judah. And besides the prophetic book that bears his name, Jeremiah also wrote the book of Lamentations.

One writer said Jeremiah was a "prophet conspicuous for his sobs and supplications, for Jeremiah knew how to pray as well as weep."[2] What may be overlooked, however, is that Jeremiah was simply, chapter after chapter, relating the *Lord's* words for Israel. If Jeremiah wept, those tears had spilled through him from the Spirit of the Lord. Let's listen in:

> I remember the devotion of your youth,
>     how as a bride you loved me
> and followed me through the wilderness,
>     through a land not sown.
>
>                         (Jer. 2:2)

> Have you not brought this on yourselves
>     by forsaking the Lord your God
>     when he led you in the way?
>
>                         (v. 17)

Why do my people say, "We are free to roam;
we will come to you no more"?

(v. 31)

The angst here in these prophetic words was actually the Lord's pain spoken through Jeremiah's mouth. Then the following were Jeremiah's words:

My eyes fail from weeping,
    I am in torment within;
my heart is poured out on the ground
    because my people are destroyed,
because children and infants faint
    in the streets of the city.

(Lam. 2:11)

This is reminiscent of Paul's writing: "Rejoice with those who rejoice, and weep with those who weep" (Rom. 12:15 NASB). Jeremiah was God's spokesman; if the Lord wept those words into Jeremiah, the prophet certainly would have wept too.

Emotive Pray-ers simply have a more sensitive nature. They're emotionally wired and feel deeply, so tears come easily as an expression of grief and heartache. When prayers come out of that sensitivity to their own or others' pain, these pray-ers find it unnatural not to cry. The key for those who naturally lament in prayer is to shift their mindset from the problem to God's provision and possibilities. We can have hope in prayer, first, because God has invited us to seek him, and second, because God is trustworthy.

## PRAYER POINTERS

- As you listen to and sing with music, think about the lyrics as your prayer.

- Allow God's Word to inspire poetic expression that you record in a journal.
- Share your own music or poetry with others.
- Journal creatively in your Bible during your prayer time.
- Pray when you're feeling emotionally heavy.
- Be brave. Share your prayer burdens with a trusted friend or family member, and allow that person to pray for you.
- Look for promises in the Bible, and turn them into prayers.
- If you have a gift for drawing or painting, use that expression to reflect your prayers.
- Create a burdens book—a journal where you write out the prayer needs of loved ones. Visualize handing them off to the Lord—let him carry that prayer-heavy yoke. Track God's answers to your prayers, which will be an encouragement to you.
- Design a "prayer closet"—a special, beautiful place that helps inspire your prayers. This could be a literal closet you have in your home or simply a cozy chair in the corner of your bedroom or living room.

## DISCUSSION QUESTIONS

1. Is prayer an emotional experience for you? Explain your answer.
2. Reread Hannah's story in 1 Samuel 1:1–20. What touches you about her prayer?
3. David wrote half of the Psalms. Which of the different kinds of psalms—laments, thanksgiving, etc.—appeals to you the most?
4. Share your favorite psalm or verse and explain why it is meaningful to you.
5. It was said of Jeremiah that he knew how to pray and how to weep. What brings you to tears when you pray?
6. Do any of the Prayer Pointers appeal to you? Which ones and why?

*Chapter 4*

# Devotional Pray-ers

You may have a friend who is so close to God that she's the first person you contact when you need others to pray. She seems to have such an other-worldly connection with the Lord that she walks and talks with him as a natural course of her day. Maybe she has said things like, "Jesus is my best friend" or "Jesus told me the most amazing thing the other day" or "God just gave me the best idea!" Devotional Pray-ers seem to always be in touch with the Lord, so much so that you might wonder if they're already halfway into heaven! Their mindset is synced with God's Word, and they see life prayerfully.

## The Friend of God: Abram/Abraham

When we have a serious prayer request, whom do we typically seek out? I text a couple friends—those I know who will stop what they're doing and pray for me. Friends stay in touch with each other, talk regularly with one another, and care for one another in meaningful ways. Dedicated friends pray faithfully. In other words, they're devoted, and Devotional Pray-ers are devoted to prayer.

We learn in James 2:23 that Abraham was "a friend of God" (NASB). That verse also says that Abraham believed God and was "righteous."

This friend of God, Abraham, was also a friend of humankind, because he was the first recorded one who interceded for others (there's no indication even Job's friends prayed for him). This man devoted to God worshipped in the manner the Lord taught him—through the offering of sacrifices (Gen. 12:7)—and he prayed several times for others:

- For his son Ishmael by Sarah's maidservant, Hagar: "If only Ishmael might live under your blessing!" (Gen. 17:18).
- Numerous times for the wicked city of Sodom, including the following: "May the Lord not be angry, but let me speak just once more. What if only ten can be found there?" (Gen. 18:32).
- For Abimelek, king of Gerar, whom Abraham had deceived: "Then Abraham prayed to God, and God healed Abimelek, his wife and his female slaves so they could have children again, for the LORD had kept all the women in Abimelek's household from conceiving because of Abraham's wife Sarah" (Gen. 20:17–18).

The first and last of the above prayers may have been motivated by Abraham's missteps—creating a child with Sarah's maidservant and trying to pass Sarah off as his sister to avoid potential violent repercussions.

But Abraham's intercession for the city of Sodom was impressive. We see a long dialogue between Abraham and the Lord, starting with God, first announcing his purpose for Abraham and then relating he would destroy Sodom and Gomorrah because of their pervasive sin. Abraham interceded for Sodom and Gomorrah. "What if there are fifty righteous people in the city?" (Gen. 18:24). And then five more times he prayed: for forty-five, forty, thirty, twenty . . . and finally, ten. The rest of the story shows that even ten righteous people couldn't be found, so the Lord destroyed the land with burning sulfur.

Devotional Pray-ers follow the Lord so closely that they appeal to him as a friend, knowing he will hear and answer their prayers. They trust God's direction implicitly and follow through with devotional practices—not out of obligation but out of devotion for the Lord they love. Devotional Pray-ers have hands wide open, extended out, as if to pray, "Here I am, Lord. Send me!" The offering of yourself and all that you love is a prayerful practice. Devotional Pray-ers are in step with God and give of themselves.

## The Thankful Poet: Deborah

The only judge also termed a prophet, Deborah held court and made decisions regarding disputes. This decisive judge became a resolute military leader as well. When the Canaanite king Jabin oppressed Deborah's people for twenty years, she took action leading ten thousand men in overcoming the enemy. While we don't hear of her pleadings with God before battle, we do see her response after winning: a chapter-long prayer that recounts the victory, starting and finishing with the following:

> When the princes in Israel take the lead,
>     when the people willingly offer themselves—
>     praise the LORD!

> Hear this, you kings! Listen, you rulers!
>     I, even I, will sing to the LORD;
>     I will praise the LORD, the God of Israel, in song.

> When you, LORD, went out from Seir,
>     when you marched from the land of Edom,
> the earth shook, the heavens poured,
>     the clouds poured down water.
> The mountains quaked before the LORD, the One of Sinai,
>     before the LORD, the God of Israel. . . .

So may all your enemies perish, LORD!
But may all who love you be like the sun
when it rises in its strength.
(Judg. 5:2–5, 31)

Simply because we only see a prayerful response here does not mean that Deborah did not pray earlier in this incident. But because of her example, we understand that responding with thanksgiving to our life challenges is a prayerful posture that takes the focus off ourselves and puts credit where credit is due: the Lord.

Devotional Pray-ers give thanksgiving in recognition of God's presence throughout all the circumstances of their lives. These thanksgivers extend appreciation for his sovereign decisions—whether they suit their fancy or not. And Devotional Pray-ers acknowledge God's many gifts. Thanksgiving prayers demonstrate a God-first perspective . . . which is one Devotional Pray-ers exemplify.

## The Word-Inspired Pray-er: Josiah

For over ten years now I've helped, and mostly recently led, a Facebook group called Bible Girls, consisting of hundreds of women who read through the Bible together each year. For the group, I post the day's reading, a Scripture-inspired meme I've created, and a prayer that has arisen out of the Scripture I've read. I allow the Word to breathe focus and meaning into the prayer. While I'm sure the prayers are not flawless, the process helps me attempt to pray according to God's Word and shifts perspective from myself and my own needs to God's truth. God's Word also inspired the prayers and life of the last godly king of Judah.

Josiah did not have godly male examples in his life. His grandfather was the evil king Manasseh, and his father, Amon, also failed to walk in the Lord's ways. His father was actually assassinated, and when those conspirators were killed, eight-year-old Josiah became the new king. Perhaps those who killed the conspirators thought they could control a young boy king. But others around him—his mother, Jedidah, and the high priest, Hilkiah—may have been more important influencers who led him to the greatest influence—the Book of the Law. This would change him and his monarchy for good and for God.

When his secretary, Shaphan, read the Book of the Covenant (which included all or portions of the Mosaic law) aloud to Josiah, the king tore his robes in repentance for his nation's not following the Lord and his commands. He then gave instructions to seek prophetic guidance (2 Kings 22:8–20). When Josiah learned that disaster would ensue for his people, he himself read the Book of the Covenant and renewed the covenant in the presence of the Lord (2 Kings 23:1–3), also leading the people to pledge themselves. That Word-inspired prayer was to "follow the LORD and keep his commands, statutes and decrees with all his heart and all his soul, thus confirming the words of the covenant written in this book" (v. 3). The Bible is compelling, and when we read it faithfully, it not only inspires our life plans but also inspires our prayer life.

Sometimes we may not fully know how to pray for a challenge in our lives. Devotional Pray-ers might open up the Word of God and pray Scriptures they have personalized for their own or others' situations. Just as the Word aligned Josiah's heart with God's covenantal expression of love and provision, the Bible will do that for us today. When our hearts are synced like a carpenter's plumb line with the Lord, biblical expression will find its way into our prayers. And when we're praying in line with God's will, God will answer our prayers.

## The Visionaries: Elisha and Jabez

With more than twenty-five years of prayerwalking accumulated on the tread of my shoes, I've seen many changes in my small town. When

I begin to make a list, it's humbling that God has allowed me to partner with my Personal Trainer (Jesus) for this work. These are just a handful of visual changes I've seen in that time:

- The demolition of a worn-down, drug-infested trailer park that blighted the west entrance to our little city of a thousand folks
- The destruction by fire of a decades-vacant, two-story hotel that has now been transformed into a fun outdoor community gathering place for local events
- Formerly vacant business shops and restaurants now beautiful places to visit
- The renovation of our little city park
- The restoration of the old, vacant middle school into a city-center building that houses city offices, an expanded and vibrant historical museum, and the best little charity thrift store in northeast California

A few years ago a former coworker who commuted to our town said, "I just love Loyalton. It's such a lovely little town." The remark stunned me because for years I had apologized for how it looked. And then I realized, *Oh, Lord, these are all answers to prayer, aren't they?*

Visionary Pray-ers pray big. In fact, their prayers may not be of their own making; instead, they may simply be conduits of the heaven-to-earth miraculous. They see things not of their imagination but of the work of God. Elisha was such a man. Elijah's protégé and successor, Elisha was also a vehicle for life-giving miracles such as the never-ending supply of oil for the poor widow (notice that her dead husband had been a prophet), the gift of a son for a childless woman (who was too humble to ask for one)—restoring that boy's life when he died—and the healing from leprosy for an army commander.[1] Notice that each of these events relates to the giving of life. While prophets often dispel doom-and-gloom scenarios, visionaries see growth and health and life.

Jabez was another visionary. His simple, one-verse prayer has become legendary:

> Jabez was more honorable than his brothers. His mother had named him Jabez, saying, "I gave birth to him in pain." Jabez cried out to the God of Israel, "Oh, that you would bless me and enlarge my territory! Let your hand be with me, and keep me from harm so that I will be free from pain." And God granted his request. (1 Chron. 4:9–10)

And that's all we know about Jabez, other than he fell into the cracks of Judah's genealogies listed in 1 Chronicles and that a city also may have been named for him (1 Chron. 2:55). One commentary offers some light on this prayer, noting that in the ancient world people often had a portentous view of life. They expected the worst. Despite Jabez's name, which means "I gave birth to him in pain," his prayer was one that hopefully countered his mother's label. He looked to God for good, for blessing, and for influence. When we pray that God's hand be with us in our purpose-driven life to serve him, we seek the best coworker possible.

Such is the prayer of Visionary Pray-ers. They see life for their families, their schools, their local governing bodies, and their communities. They expect God to do the miraculous. They live out their faith looking up. Am I such a pray-er? Perhaps. One morning very early in my prayerwalking experience, I approached and read our city limits sign.

LOYALTON

Pop. 1,180    Elev. 4,980

I stopped in thought. What if it instead read:

LOYALTON

A Place Where God Lives

Now where did that thought come from? Me? I don't think so. But I imagined a newcomer entering our town for the first time, meeting the friendly, kind local folks, and just wondering what it was that made our town so different. He stops at the local grocery store to buy a soda and asks the clerk, "What makes this town so different?"

And the clerk says, "Well, Loyalton is A Place Where God Lives."

A similar vision came to me some years later—that a church would exist someday in each of the corners of our valley. Since then, two churches have been founded in those missing corners.

Visionary Pray-ers see possibilities—those impossible, life-giving God Things coming to fruition. And then those things do come true. Mark Batterson writes, "It's the impossible prayers that honor God because they reveal our faith and allow God to reveal His glory."[2] If you pray BIG, reader friend, you may be a Visionary Pray-er. Keep praying big. Keep praying beyond your own reach . . . and just see what God may do.

## The Disciplined Pray-er: Daniel

In *PrayerWalk* I jokingly relate how I have wrestled with the *d* word: discipline. Exercise routines have been tried and discarded. Prayer routines have come and gone. Prayer journals, prayer lists, and prayer notebooks have all gone the way of most New Year's resolutions . . . unfinished. While other disciplines such as reading my Bible daily and prayerwalking have become routine, I still see myself as someone weak in the prayer arena. I am not a Daniel.

When Darius the Mede slipped into leadership in Babylon after the Persian takeover, advisers said he should issue an edict prohibiting anyone from praying to any man or god for the next thirty days, punishable by death. Darius agreed. However, Daniel, who had been in leadership, continued his practice of praying to the Lord God.

Now when Daniel learned that the decree had been published, he went home to his upstairs room where the windows opened toward Jerusalem. Three times a day he got down on his knees and prayed, giving thanks to his God, *just as he had done before.* (Dan. 6:10, emphasis added)

Three times a day Daniel went to prayer—whether it was legal or not. Was this a legalistic practice or Daniel's personal discipline? David mentioned prayer at evening, morning, and noon in Psalm 55:17. The Levites, who formed the Jewish priesthood, were to stand every morning and every evening to thank and praise the Lord (1 Chron. 23:30). And we find references to both standing and kneeling in prayer in the Old Testament (Neh. 9:2, 5; 1 Kings 8:54). Daniel's prayer disciplines seem to have been of his own conviction, as he was also disciplined in personal behavior—not drinking anything but water and not eating anything but vegetables. He stuck to his prayerful practices, even going to the lions' den rather than follow edicts meant to inhibit his faith.

I know people like this. They immediately go to their Bibles in the morning with their cup of java in hand—studying for a certain period of time, reflecting in their journals, praying over long lists of prayer needs, and sitting quietly as they wait for a possible word from God that they write down. I have the greatest admiration for them and can see the spiritual fruit in their lives—faith that seasons with years despite the storms that rage and go.

I have systematic routines for Bible study; I read and journal through the Bible each year, create inspirational memes that I post online in a half dozen places, and daily write a reflective blog about what I think God is teaching me. But my prayer practices differ—they are responsive to what occurs around me and what faces me ahead. And I have peace with that. Now . . . if I could only settle for just vegetables!

—————————— PRAYER POINTERS ——————————

- Allow prayer to live in the moment—praying your way throughout your day.

- Thank God for every circumstance and thing that comes your way, as well as the people around you.
- Ask God for his next steps for you.
- Confess your sins as they occur, so you can stay close to God.
- Use God's Word as a springboard for prayer.
- Memorize Scripture so it can form your prayers.
- Notice others' needs and pray for them . . . and with them.
- Don't forget to pray for what you need.
- Consider prayerwalking as a devotional practice. It may help you understand that wherever you are, there's a need for prayer.
- Pray BIG, vision-inspired prayers for your community.
- Consider a regular practice of fasting for the purpose of focused prayer for some kind of breakthrough.

## DISCUSSION QUESTIONS

1. Whom do you know who is so in touch with the Lord that she or he seems to be praying without ceasing?
2. Why do you think Abraham was called "friend of God" (James 2:23 NASB)?
3. Read the Song of Deborah in Judges 5. How did Deborah give thanks?
4. How did the Word of God inspire Josiah's prayer life?
5. The prayer of Jabez found in 1 Chronicles 4:9–10 has become well known. Summarize it in your own words, and share how you think God might enlarge your "territory."
6. What benefits do you find from Daniel's disciplined prayer life?
7. Do any of the Prayer Pointers appeal to you? Which ones and why?

*Chapter* 5

# Physical Pray-ers

My daughter's oldest and my son's oldest couldn't be more different. Even as a little boy, upon entering our home Josiah would sit down on the couch or at the kitchen counter and say, "So, how's your day been, Nana?" He values relationships and loves rich conversation. In contrast, Dillan's first question might be, "Can I play the Wii, Nana?" He is happiest when physically active and looks for new ways to test his body.

We do not pray apart from our bodies, do we? Even if we're completely silent, our minds, hearts, and souls are fixed on the Lord. We use our mouths to give praise and thanksgiving and to ask God for what is on our hearts. So, yes, all prayer has a physical nature, but some people put more of their physical selves into the practice.

Physical Pray-ers connect with God in corporal (bodily) ways, including prayerwalking, using a labyrinth, kneeling for prayer, and even subjugating the body through the practice of fasting. This chapter will examine several people who approached God in physical ways: Jacob, Joshua, and a trio of fasters—Ezra, Nehemiah, and Esther.

## The Wrestler: Jacob

The fact that Jacob literally wrestled with God is an indicator of his physical prayer posture, and we can learn about the importance of persistence in prayer from him. Jacob knew something of struggles. He figuratively wrestled with his older brother, Esau, to snatch away his birthright, and then his father-in-law, Laban, made Jacob work for him twenty years before he could set out on his own with his wives Leah and Rachel, as well as his maidservants and flocks. Returning to the land of Esau, Jacob knew he would have to face the brother he had cheated. But he wasn't prepared to wrestle with God through that evening until daybreak, suffering a hip dislocation in the process.

This dialogue (Gen. 32:26–30) shows Jacob's negotiating prowess:

> Then the man said, "Let me go, for it is daybreak."
>
> But Jacob replied, "I will not let you go unless you bless me."
>
> The man asked him, "What is your name?"
>
> "Jacob," he answered.
>
> Then the man said, "Your name will no longer be Jacob, but Israel, because you have struggled with God and with humans and have overcome."
>
> Jacob said, "Please tell me your name."
>
> But he replied, "Why do you ask my name?" Then he blessed him there.
>
> So Jacob called the place Peniel, saying, "It is because I saw God face to face, and yet my life was spared."

We, too, may feel we wrestle with God in prayer. We pray continually for a family member to come to the faith. We pray night and day for a kid making bad decisions. We pray for a breakthrough in our health or work situation or sick friend. Such prayer feels like work, and Wrestlers may even pace the floor or go to their knees. There are some evenings or early mornings I feel impelled to pray from my knees, which I jokingly call my "kneeler knees" from my formal church liturgy background. This physical act of submission in prayer seems to emphasize my prayer's importance and somehow gives me peace as I turn over the need to the Lord.

After Jacob's nightlong wrestling match with the Lord God, he "passes 'from the boldness of self-confidence to the boldness of faith,' and becomes Israel, the Prince of God. The Hand that touched Jacob's sinew, touched his soul and changed the supplanter into a saint."[1] Ultimately, the purpose of prayer is fellowship with the Lord God, and that fellowship—whether it's a wrestling prayer match, or intercession from our knees, or even prostration on the floor—changes me from someone who tries to grab more than I deserve into someone more like the Lord I serve.

## The Obedient Listener: Joshua

Some adults are just better listeners than others. They listen to their friends and family, weigh their words, and respond with succinct statements. Some children are better listeners than others too. Years ago, if I asked two of our kids to clean their rooms, they'd procrastinate until threatened with grounding. The other two were compliant: if I asked them to do the dishes, the dishes were done.

Listening was a strength and prayer style of Moses's successor, Joshua, a servant in prayer. The Lord gave him instructions about how to lead the people across the Jordan and into their various assigned areas by tribe, and Joshua listened and obeyed. Almost without exception, we don't hear objections from Joshua or back-and-forth conversation as we did with Moses. Joshua, one of the twelve spies who scouted out the promised land, was one of only two who returned enthusiastically ready to conquer the inhabited territories.

After Moses died, the Lord gave Joshua the charge to lead the Israelites. He repeated "be strong and courageous" three times and told Joshua, "Keep this Book of the Law always on your lips; meditate on it day and night, so that you may be careful to do everything written in it" (Josh. 1:8). Joshua's response? We have not one recorded word to this initial direction from God. Instead, we see Joshua immediately putting orders into effect to the various tribes' officers. Joshua listened and obeyed the Lord. Obedience was his prayer style.

Let's look at several directives of the Lord to Joshua:

The Lord: "Tell the priests who carry the ark of the covenant, 'When you reach the edge of the Jordan's waters, go and stand in the river.'" (Josh. 3:8)
Joshua: "Come here and listen to the words of the LORD your God." (v. 9)

The Lord: "Choose twelve men from among the people, one from each tribe . . ." (Josh. 4:2)
Joshua: So Joshua called together the twelve men he had appointed from the Israelites, one from each tribe . . . (v. 4)

The Lord: "See, I have delivered Jericho into your hands, along with its king and its fighting men. March around the city once with all the armed men. Do this for six days." (Josh. 6:2–3)
Joshua: So Joshua son of Nun . . . ordered the army, "Advance!" (vv. 6–7)

Only once do we hear a complaint from Joshua to the Lord God. One of the Israelites, Achan, stole riches from Canaan in direct opposition to the Lord's and Joshua's commands. When the Lord allowed a significant loss in battle as a consequence for Achan's sin, Joshua prayed, "Alas, Sovereign LORD, why did you ever bring this people across the Jordan to deliver us into the hands of the Amorites to destroy us? If only we had been content to stay on the other side of the Jordan!" (Joshua 7:7).

In response the Lord said, "Stand up! What are you doing down on your face? Israel has sinned; they have violated my covenant, which I commanded them to keep" (vv. 10–11). Moving into action is a prayerful response for Physical Pray-ers, who may not have much to say and may not petition God for their own needs. In other instances of God's direction, Joshua heard God and moved to respond. Joshua listened. And Joshua's prayerful response was obedience.

You might not feel you talk enough to God. But you read the Bible, you wait for his direction, and you follow his leading. Others might observe that you're a good person—a good child of God. You might not think so, though. You just do what you're told and feel prayerfully knit with the God you love and serve. In other words, you are a Physical Pray-er.

## The Fasting Pray-ers: Ezra, Nehemiah, Esther

Fasting can bring about spiritual breakthrough, and many biblical characters fasted as they prayed for change and strength. While some see it as an optional spiritual discipline in current times, Jesus emphasized its importance and the right mindset in the Sermon on the Mount:

> When you fast, do not look somber as the hypocrites do, for they disfigure their faces to show others they are fasting. Truly I tell you, they have received their reward in full. But when you fast, put oil on your head and wash your face, so that it will not be obvious to others that you are fasting, but only to your Father, who is unseen; and your Father, who sees what is done in secret, will reward you. (Matt. 6:16–18)

Notice Jesus's use of the word *when* twice: *"when* you fast" (emphasis added). Before he began his ministry, Jesus fasted in the desert and overcame Satan's temptations (Luke 4). Fasting, Elmer L. Towns writes, "could shake our society like a windstorm bending a sapling. Christians would demonstrate that they live differently, that their faith is imperative, that the Almighty works in their daily lives."[2] We can see how God worked in the lives of three biblical people through prayer and fasting: Ezra, Nehemiah, and Esther.

After some of the Israelites returned to Jerusalem from exile in Babylon and rebuilt the temple, Ezra, "a teacher well versed in the Law of Moses," arrived to teach (Ezra 7:6). After gathering the people to return, Ezra called for a fast, explaining,

> There, by the Ahava Canal, I proclaimed a fast, so that we might humble ourselves before our God and ask him for a safe journey for us and our children, with all our possessions. I was ashamed to ask the king for soldiers and horsemen to protect us from enemies on the road, because we had told the king, "The gracious hand of our God is on everyone who looks to him, but his great anger is against all who forsake him." So we fasted and petitioned our God about this, and he answered our prayer. (Ezra 8:21–23)

With fasting one intensifies prayer. Instead of taking time to prepare and eat food, people spend that time in prayer. Ezra also fasted in prayer later when he learned of the people's intermarriage, which would lead the remaining Jews into the religions of other gods (Ezra 10:6). While the earlier fast was for favor from King Artaxerxes in Babylon, the latter fast was to mourn the apostasy of the remnant.

Many people today fast—but not many actually do so for prayer-related reasons. Typically, when we hear of someone fasting, it's for a dietary lifestyle change to lose weight. Towns writes that the Bible teaches there are numerous spiritual reasons to fast and pray:

- To find freedom from addiction (Matt. 17:20, 21)[3]
- To solve problems (Ezra 8:21–23)
- To win people to Christ (1 Sam. 7:1–8)
- To break crippling fears and other mental problems (1 Kings 19:2–8)
- To provide for the needy (1 Kings 17:12)
- To gain insight for decision-making (Acts 9:9–19)
- To have better health and physical healing (Dan. 1:12–20)
- To prepare for an influential testimony (Matt. 3:4; Luke 1:15)
- To seek protection from the evil one (Esther 4:16)[4]

There seems to be a connection between our making sacrifices and God's answering our prayers. Again, it may be that our hearts, in fact, begin to align more with our Lord's so that our prayers become "thy will be done."

Nehemiah, who returned from exile to repair the protective walls around Jerusalem, fasted as well. Many instances of spontaneous prayers in response to difficulties are recorded in the book of Nehemiah, with two accompanied by fasting. First, when he initially learned of the condition of the walls, he "mourned and fasted and prayed" before the Lord (Neh. 1:4–11). This prayer sought clarity of direction about what to do, and as a result King Artaxerxes not only allowed him to return but even equipped him with protective soldiers and materials.

Nehemiah's other instance of fasting happened in Jerusalem when the Israelites gathered, "fasting and wearing sackcloth and putting dust on their heads" in an act of repentance and rededication to God (Neh. 9:1). Nehemiah's legacy is one not only of work with the restoration of the wall, but also of prayer and fasting. The people of God had to be retrained in the things of the Lord, and Nehemiah and Ezra led them in those spiritual disciplines.

Another Old Testament figure who taught the importance and efficacy of fasting is Esther. Shortly after the Hebrew woman was named queen of Susa in Persia (prior to the time of Ezra and Nehemiah), she learned of an evil plot by Haman, the king's official, to annihilate all the Jews in the kingdom. When her relative Mordecai urged her to appeal to the king, she responded as follows:

> Go, gather together all the Jews who are in Susa, and fast for me. Do not eat or drink for three days, night or day. I and my attendants will fast as you do. When this is done, I will go to the king, even though it is against the law. And if I perish, I perish. (Esther 4:16)

While the entire book of Esther does not contain the words *pray* or *prayer*, fasting was a spiritual practice that, in Jewish tradition, was accompanied by prayer. Esther fasted for protection, because at that time if she approached the king without having been summoned, she could be put to death. Fasting likely also gave her wisdom about what to do and what to say. The results? We learn from the story that the king welcomed her and granted her petition to reverse his earlier edict that would've annihilated all the Jews in the land.

Many fast today for personal breakthrough and the breakdown of negative spiritual strongholds. Occasionally, I will fast from certain kinds of foods, such as those with caffeine and sweets and those with simple carbohydrates. With each of those fasts I find greater clarity for direction and problem-solving, as well as answers to prayer. When one of my children was in crisis, I fasted for several days, praying often instead of prepping or eating food. And God answered my prayers for that child. I also have a friend who fasts from everything except fruits and vegetables for the month of January as she prayerfully seeks direction for the coming year. Each year she reports feeling stronger physically, mentally, emotionally, and spiritually. Fasting plus prayer is an effectual practice.

## PRAYER POINTERS

- Walk while you pray. Take your prayer requests to the streets or to your treadmill. Listen to worship music and pray for those situations and people on your mental prayer list.
- Try a prayerwalk. Prayerwalking is different than walking while praying. Prayerwalking is an intercessory practice that inspires you to pray for the needs of others in the homes, schools, businesses, and governmental offices you pass. Ask God for insight, and he will increase your awareness of those prayer needs.
- At home bow your head, raise your hands, kneel, or lie prostrate on your stomach while you pray.
- Praise God through dance to worship music.
- Try labyrinthian prayer. If there's not a labyrinth in your area, you can make one with rocks from your yard. Someone in our church neighborhood created one in an unused part of the parking lot. Give yourself over to the Lord as you slowly walk to the very middle of the labyrinth—in confession and submission. Then listen to God and receive his affirmation and direction as you slowly walk back out to the starting point.
- Pay attention to your senses: touch, taste, smell, hearing, and sight. Respond in prayer. Even if you sense physical pain, give thanks.
- Respond with acts of obedience. Let your good works be prayerful offerings to God.
- Consider fasting. Check with your doctor to see if you can abstain from everything except water for a given period of time. Or

give up one meal such as breakfast or dinner—using the time you'd be prepping food for additional time in prayer.

## DISCUSSION QUESTIONS

1. Have you ever felt as though you were wrestling with God in prayer because you've just prayed so long for that answer? Explain how that has felt.
2. React to the statement, "Obedience was [Joshua's] prayer style."
3. The one time Joshua complained to the Lord, the Lord said, "Stand up! What are you doing down on your face?" (Josh. 7:10). How do you feel about the Lord's response to Joshua?
4. How do you feel about fasting? Is that something you've done?
5. What are the spiritual benefits of fasting?
6. How were Nehemiah's and Esther's fasts similar?
7. Do any of the Prayer Pointers appeal to you? Which ones and why?

# Chapter 6

# Jesus, the Model for Prayer

MORE THAN TWO DECADES AGO when I began studying prayer in the Bible, what I noticed most through those pages from Genesis to Revelation was that God, the Creator of heaven and earth and all living things, pursued a relationship with humankind. Good relationships require communication. Just as a marriage will suffer if we don't take time to talk to each other daily, our relationship with the Lord will stagnate or even fade away if we make ourselves too busy and the Lord too unimportant.

God initiated conversation with the men and women of the Bible. The first recorded spoken words in the Bible are God speaking to Adam and Eve: "Be fruitful and increase in number" (Gen. 1:28). He spoke to the patriarchs, the judges, and the kings and then directly to larger audiences through the prophets. However, the people stopped listening and turned a deaf ear to God, so we have what are called the "silent years." Because of the lack of prophetic revelation or inspired, historical recordings, there were about four hundred "silent" years from the time of Nehemiah and the last prophet, Malachi, to the coming of Christ.

If prayer is meant to develop our relationship with the Lord God, the best news was yet to come: God would come to earth in human form so that we might understand his character, his love, and his plan for humanity's salvation. Jesus said, "I have come into the world as a light, so that no one who believes in me should stay in darkness" (John 12:46). When we don't have communication, we simply don't know what is true.

In Jesus we see a praying lifestyle lived out in full. Jesus's life brings light to our understanding of who God is and how to pray. In other words, he is our Model Pray-er. Specifically, we will look at Jesus's prayers, what he did as prayer practices, and his teachings related to prayer.

## Jesus's Prayers

When we pray, we often focus our prayers on our needs or those of ones we love. But the ten prayers of Jesus recorded in Scripture demonstrate a wider perspective. We certainly see him responding to others' needs, as well as his own, but he includes prayers for daily needs and of praise, thanksgiving, adoration, petition, intercession, forgiveness, lament, and relinquishment.

While many have attempted to create a personality profile for Jesus, I do not believe this is appropriate. Scripture tells us, "When the set time had fully come, God sent his Son, born of a woman, born under the law, to redeem those under the law, that we might receive adoption to sonship" (Gal. 4:4–5). Jesus is the Son of God. The Son of God is God the Son. God the Son would have a perfect or complete personality. While he experienced life in the flesh, including its temptations, he responded as God the Son. So Jesus was as much one kind of personality as another.

To use just one personality assessment as an example, here are some thoughts:

- Was he an introvert or extrovert? Both. He welcomed the masses for teaching and healing, but he found moments of solitude up the mountain to pray.
- Did he take in information by sensing or intuition? Both. He quickly assessed situations around him, but he also knew bigger picture, eternal connections.

- Did he make decisions through thinking or feeling? Both. He reasonably and quickly found flaws in arguments, but he also was empathetic.
- Did he live his outer life from a judging or perceiving perspective? Both. He understood the Father's purpose (plans, rules, timing) for his coming to earth, but he also responded to spontaneous situations around him.

It's natural that Jesus's collective personality would play out through his prayer life; and so his life provides a praying model for us.

## Petition

The first of Jesus's ten prayers found in the Gospels is the Lord's Prayer, found in Matthew 6:9–13 (with an alternate version in Luke 11:2–4). The parts break down like this:

| Verse | Text | Prayer Type |
|-------|------|-------------|
| 9 | Our Father in heaven, hallowed be your name, | Praise |
| 10 | your kingdom come, your will be done, on earth as it is in heaven. | Relinquishment/ Submission |
| 11 | Give us today our daily bread. | Petition |
| 12 | And forgive us our debts, as we also have forgiven our debtors. | Petition: Forgiveness/ Confession |
| 13 | And lead us not into temptation, but deliver us from the evil one. | Petition: Deliverance |

The Lord's Prayer is a model—Jesus's response to the disciples when they said, "Lord, teach us to pray" (Luke 11:1). His example shows it is perfectly all right to ask for daily needs but important to first recognize the holiness of God and his perfect plan and also live out a life of for-giveness and obedience.

Most of us have probably heard that our prayers should be ordered: praise, confess, give thanks, and *then* supplicate (or ask). But notice here that Jesus sticks the "ask" in the middle of his model prayer. Richard Foster notes that Jesus included the "give" portion of the prayer before the "forgive" portion. He writes,

> If we were not so familiar with the Lord's Prayer, we would be astonished at the petition for daily bread. If it had come from the lips of any other than Jesus himself, we would consider it an intrusion of materialism upon the refined realm of prayer. But here it is smack in the greatest of prayers: "Give us this day our daily bread."
>
> When we think about it for a moment, though, we realize that this prayer is completely consistent with Jesus' pattern of living, for he occupied himself with the trivialities of human-kind . . . he welcomes us with our 1,001 trifles, for they are each important to him.[1]

Bottom line: it's okay to ask—even just for daily needs. And if you ask a lot, that's all right too—you're going to the right place.

### Praise

A two-sentence Jesus prayer—sometimes called the Galilean prayer—is often overlooked. Sandwiched between woes and "my yoke is easy," it reads:

> At that time Jesus said, "I praise you, Father, Lord of heaven and earth, because you have hidden these things from the wise and learned, and revealed them to little children. Yes, Father, for this is what you were pleased to do." (Matt. 11:25–26)

It's an odd praise, isn't it? Connected to the earlier and following verses, however, the prayer makes sense. Just prior to this Jesus had denounced several towns (Korazin, Bethsaida, Tyre, Sidon, Capernaum) because even though he'd done miracles in them, the people still did not believe in him. Jesus acknowledged God's position as "Lord of heaven and earth" and allowed his praise to magnify his Father's sovereignty.

When things don't go our way and when people get in our way, it's easy to complain to sideliners instead of praying. Instead, the practice of praising God and acknowledging his perfect will lifts us up emotionally too. Jesus took his resentment and frustration and turned it into praise.

## Thanksgiving

What may be my favorite of Jesus's prayers occurs right before he raises Lazarus from the dead (see John 11:44). The brother of Mary and Martha of Bethany, Lazarus, died. Jesus knew them well because they'd hosted him when he was in that area near Jerusalem. Even though Jesus initially heard Lazarus was sick, he delayed traveling to their home for two days—knowing then that Lazarus was dead (vv. 14–15).

When Jesus arrived in Bethany, he went to the tomb, had the stone rolled away from the entrance, and looking up, prayed, "Father, I thank you that you have heard me. I knew that you always hear me, but I said this for the benefit of the people standing here, that they may believe that you sent me" (vv. 41–42).

Then Jesus spoke, "Lazarus, come out!" (v. 43). And Lazarus walked out from the tomb.

Jesus responded, "Take off the grave clothes and let him go" (v. 44).

I love this prayer, because it shows me that I should not only give thanks for what I have; I should also thank the Lord for what he *will* do in the future. It expresses appreciation but also absolute faith. This kind of thanksgiving prayer is not a name-it-claim-it one, asking for a lottery win: it celebrates what God has done in my life and expresses my utmost trust that I can step into God's future provision and blessing—knowing that his presence in my life is better than any present I could receive. It balances life and death on a life scale: if I am not resurrected from the problem God has allowed in my life, I am still wholly in the trustworthy grip of his hands.

## Adoration

Another oft-missed prayer from Jesus is found in the next chapter of John—a prayer that demonstrates the posture of adoration, one of reverent worship. As I pray throughout my church on Sundays prior to our worship service, I often pray, "Lord, be glorified and honored and praised in whatever we say, do, and even think today." That is expressing adoration for the God of the universe. Jesus did this too, after his triumphal entry into Jerusalem for the last time.

As a king would do, Jesus rode on a donkey into a path of laid-down palm branches on a day we now call Palm Sunday. The people raised loud hosannas to him. And while Jesus's disciples might have thought Jesus was headed to the literal throne of the kingdom, he knew what was ahead. He prayed,

> Now my soul is troubled, and what shall I say? "Father, save me from this hour"? No, it was for this very reason I came to this hour. Father, glorify your name! (John 12:27–28)

The disciples thought Jesus would be enthroned, raised up, and glorified by the masses. But Jesus simply wanted his Father's name glorified. This is ultimate worship—the setting aside of self and personal ambition for adoration of God. Jesus and the Father were one, but he still offered adoration to his Father in heaven.

Does God need praise? Even C. S. Lewis struggled with this question, wondering why the Creator would need admiration. But then his wrestlings settled into an understanding that in the process of worship, God communicates his presence to men. "What had escaped [Lewis's] notice is the notion that all enjoyment spontaneously overflows into praise."[2] As we spend more time with God, our prayers will turn more toward adoration.

### Petition

When we sign a petition, we indicate we want something to change. We have a need and put our official name to a document indicating that need is important to us. Petitionary prayer is asking God for something we need: daily needs (food, shelter, financial provision), better marriages, restoration of other relationships, healing, guidance. We have a condition in our lives that troubles us, and we need that situation to change.

Jesus prayed for himself several times; the first of those prayers seen in John 17 is often called the Priestly Prayer. The longest of his prayers, it fills a chapter and is typically divided into three parts: prayer for himself, prayer for his disciples, and prayer for others who would come to faith in him. The petitionary part of the prayer is in the first five verses, when he prays for himself:

> Father, the hour has come. Glorify your Son, that your Son may glorify you. For you granted him authority over all people that he might give eternal life to all those you have given him. Now this is eternal life: that they know you, the only true God, and Jesus Christ, whom you have sent. I have brought you glory on earth by finishing the work you gave me to do. And now, Father, glorify me in your presence with the glory I had with you before the world began. (vv. 1–5)

Jesus specifically asked that he be glorified, so others would know his heavenly Father sent him and glorify the Father through their own faith. That's a perfect prayer right there: "Raise me up, God, only for the purpose of others turning toward you."

The Greek word for *glorify* here is *doxazō*, which means "to do honor to or to make glorious."[3] However, Jesus did not ask to be made more than what he was on earth. If he were glorified, others would recognize him for who he was—the Christ, the Messiah, the Son of God. He did not ask to be made king but that others would see his glory as Emmanuel, God With Us. Jesus asked for what he needed; we can too.

## Intercession

The rest of the Priestly Prayer is for others. First, Jesus prayed for his disciples—for their protection, for the full measure of Christ's joy within them, and for their sanctification by God's Word. Those words in John 17:6–19 are what a parent would pray for their child—for their safety, for happiness in life, and for a lifetime of faith as they seek to live out God's Word in their lives.

Then Jesus shifted to pray for "those who will believe in me through their message" (v. 20), asking for their unity, their witness to the world, their future heavenly reunion with Christ, and God's love for them. With this part of the prayer, it's humbling to think Jesus was praying for you and for me. It calls to mind how mothers and fathers pray for the future spouses of their children. Jesus prayed for centuries-to-come believers, and now we have the opportunity to pray for others and serve God in unity and love so as to fulfill that prayer.

## Relinquishment

Jesus's three Gethsemane Garden petitions represent the relinquishment prayer—like the "your will be done" prayer we say in the Lord's Prayer. Here are the three versions of the first prayer:

My Father, if it is possible, may this cup be taken from me. Yet not as I will, but as you will. (Matt. 26:39)

*Abba*, Father . . . everything is possible for you. Take this cup from me. Yet not what I will, but what you will. (Mark 14:36)

Father, if you are willing, take this cup from me; yet not my will, but yours be done. (Luke 22:42)

Only Matthew records the second of Jesus's Gethsemane prayers:

My Father, if it is not possible for this cup to be taken away unless I drink it, may your will be done. (Matt. 26:42)

Two of the writers report that Jesus prayed a third prayer, but we do not have its wording.

This may be the best human prayer we can pray. In this prayer we know that Jesus is fully God and fully man. He prayed for his most human desire: life. And yet he prayed for God's will to be done through him. In an earlier book I called these the "two-sided coin prayers."[4] One side of the prayer represents the "head"—what I want. The other side of the prayer represents the "tail"—the bigger, God picture. And the prayer is called a relinquishment prayer because we relinquish what we want for the better plan, God's will.

### Forgiveness

The Lord's Prayer already shows us Jesus considers forgiveness an important part of our daily prayers: asking forgiveness for ourselves and giving it for others who have offended us. But we have an even greater visual of the forgiveness prayer in the first of Jesus's three prayers from the cross. Jesus prayed, "Father, forgive them, for they do not know what they are doing" (Luke 23:34). Of any prayer, this one articulates the whole purpose of his going to the cross: the forgiveness of our sins. It's significant, I believe, that this is the first of his cross prayers. Before he asked anything for himself, he forgave the soldiers who arrested him, nailed him, divided up his clothes . . . and perhaps also those who condemned him, abandoned him, and betrayed him. This is a fully Jesus-as-God prayer uttered through his human lips. Oh, that I could pray such a prayer, fully mean it, and live it out.

### Forsaken Prayer

The second cross prayer is a lament and represents what we all pray at some time—no matter our personality: *Why, God?* Scripture says, "And at three in the afternoon Jesus cried out in a loud voice, *'Eloi, Eloi, lema sabachthani?'* (which means 'My God, my God, why have you forsaken me?')" (Mark 15:34). It is a natural, human response to life's pain to cry out to God, questioning the *whys* behind our suffering. The Gethsemane prayers of relinquishment showed us Jesus's willingness to suffer on the cross, but this lament shows that we can also question God's will and cry out in prayer.

### Submission

The last of Jesus's ten prayers is found only in Luke 23:46: "Father, into your hands I commit my spirit." Jesus had healed the lame and the blind and the sick. He had also resurrected others from death. He could have removed himself from the cross and walked away. But in this prayer of submission, he chose to submit or release himself fully into the Father's hands.

I picture a child struggling in a parent's embrace. She so badly wants to do what she wants to do—run away in that grocery store or at that amusement park. But eventually she fully understands the safety in her father's arms and stops the struggle. Jesus stopped the struggle and prayed for his release of earth's grip . . . not for his benefit but for ours.

Some personalities struggle with control and want to be able to orchestrate every detail. They find it hard to let go and trust their outcome to the unknown. The first chapter of John's Gospel tells us that the world was made through the Word, Jesus. With a word Jesus could have chosen a drastically different course. Instead, our Emmanuel—God With Us—uttered a prayer that changed our course of history. His prayer put himself into the Father's hands, allowing us the same opportunity.

## Jesus's Prayer Practices

We also learn about Jesus's prayer life from his actual practices of prayer. People can talk a lot about prayer (throw me in that bunch), but a praying life is one that provides evidence of looking up. In the Gospels we see Jesus sometimes used Scripture in his prayers, prayed at all times of the day, prayed in remote spots away from the crowds but also in front of them, provided blessings and thanksgiving, and agonized in prayer.

Praying Scripture, as Jesus often did, provides several benefits. When we incorporate verses from the Bible in our prayers (used contextually and correctly), we bring the authority and power of God's Word into our communication with the Lord. When Jesus fasted in the desert for forty days prior to shifting into his ministry, he used Scripture three times to refute Satan's temptations (Matt. 4:1–11; Mark 1:12–13; Luke 4:1–13). Fasting shifts our whole being from an earthly focus to a heavenly perspective, particularly when we use God's Word. While the words *pray* or *prayer* are not used in these passages, it was a common Jewish practice that prayer accompanied fasting.

Jesus incorporated Scripture at other times in his prayers as well; of note is his reference to Psalm 22:1 with his "My God, my God, why have you forsaken me?" prayer from the cross. Praying Scripture has two other benefits: it helps us when we don't know how to pray, and it helps us pray more closely into God's will for a situation. Those who have the personality type that needs to get things exactly right might find it helpful to pray God's Word as they read it or turn to it when confused.

Where and when did Jesus pray? He prayed openly in front of others and remotely on his own (Matt. 14:13). He blessed children and gave thanks for the meager food offerings at the feedings of the five thousand and four thousand (Matt. 15:36; Mark 6:41; 8:7; Luke 9:16; John 6:11). This thanksgiving was to God, not merely the contributors, because two of the Gospel writers reported Jesus looking up before giving thanks. He prayed before the disciples in the upper room (John 17) and in response to the disciples' request to teach them to pray (Luke 11:1). Like Jesus, perhaps you also respond prayerfully when needs are placed in front of you.

He also prayed alone for long stretches. After dismissing the disciples to move ahead of him in the boat to the other side of the Sea of Galilee, "he went up on a mountainside by himself to pray" (Matt. 14:23) and apparently was there until the fourth watch (3:00 a.m. to 6:00 a.m.), when he walked on water to meet up with them again. Mark recorded that Jesus arose while it was still dark and went to a solitary place to pray (Mark 1:35). The night before he called the twelve disciples, he prayed all night long on a mountainside (Luke 6:12). And we read "Jesus often withdrew to lonely places and prayed" (Luke 5:16). Those closest to him knew he often prayed—early in the morning or through an evening.

Jesus also agonized in prayer. Luke, a physician, wrote that when Jesus prayed for a period of time in the Gethsemane Garden, an "angel from heaven appeared to him and strengthened him" and his anguish was so great, his sweat was like "drops of blood falling to the ground" (Luke 22:43–44). Jesus labored in prayer, as his life was in the balance. Those who have prayed long stretches in hospital waiting rooms know the exhaustion that can set in because of the emotion expended appealing to the Lord of the life scales.

## Jesus's Teachings on Prayer

Jesus also taught about prayer. In fact, the subject of prayer in his teachings was only secondary to that of eternal life. Here are summaries of those teachings:

- Pray in a private setting, not publicly if our motive is to impress others (Matt. 6:5–6).
- Pray simply and succinctly. There's no need for prayers to go on and on because God knows our needs (Matt. 6:7–13; Mark 12:40).
- Pray forgiveness when others offend us because God forgives us (Matt. 6:14–15).
- Be watchful in prayer so as not to fall into temptation (Matt. 26:41; Mark 14:38; Luke 22:45–46). Be active and alert in prayer.
- Pray for healing because some healings may only come about through prayer (Mark 9:14–29).
- Pray boldly (Luke 11:5–13). I like to say we should pray "beyond our reach."
- Pray persistently (Luke 18:1–8). God wants us to be faithful in prayer—not give up but instead persist.

Jesus clearly taught that prayer is vital to one's very being and should be prioritized. He taught that prayer is a natural outpouring of our relationship with God, so we need not stumble over words or make attempts to impress him or even others. We serve a big God, so taking our big needs and requests to him is perfectly all right. Of course, Jesus's praying style would have been natural because he and the Father were one, but his example shows us that we, too, can approach the living God simply and yet boldly over and over again—whether that is natural to our personality or not.

## ——— PRAYER POINTERS ———

- See prayer as the opportunity to develop a personal relationship with the triune God: Father, Son, and Spirit.
- View prayer as an all-day conversation.
- Pray at sunup and sundown.
- See people as opportunities and reasons for prayer.
- Seek time away from the world in your own version of a prayer

closet—somewhere you can go to be undisturbed. Susanna Wesley, mother of the great evangelists John and Charles Wesley, pulled an apron over her head and prayed while her ten children read or played around her.[5]

- See life within a framework of prayer—with continual opportunities for intercession and petition.
- Use God's Word to help form your prayers.
- Offer prayers of praise and thanksgiving in response to your surroundings. Thank God for his provision—even before you have received it.
- Offer prayers of blessing for meals and people you meet, as well as their homes.
- Forgive immediately and give up resentments and bitterness.
- Open your hands and give yourself up in submission to God's plan for your life . . . each day as you are blessed with yet another one.

## DISCUSSION QUESTIONS

1. Why is prayer important, according to the chapter introduction?
2. What are your thoughts about personality qualities in Jesus?
3. What do we learn about prayer from the Lord's Prayer in Matthew 6:9-13?
4. How could you incorporate more praise and thanksgiving in your prayer times?
5. Petitionary prayers are those we pray for ourselves. Intercessory prayers are those said for others. What should be a healthy balance between the two, do you think?
6. What is some of your takeaway from the section on Jesus's teachings on prayer?
7. Do any of the Prayer Pointers appeal to you? Which ones and why?

*Chapter 7*

# Paul, the On-the-Run Intercessor

WE THINK OF THE APOSTLE Paul as an enthusiastic missionary to the Gentiles, the non-Jews. We think of him as a discipler, exhorter, letter writer, and teacher. But he was also an intercessor who faithfully prayed for those who followed Jesus as a result of his teachings. His home was on the road, and from his conversion story in Acts and his thirteen letters to churches and individuals, we see that he prayed as God brought others to mind.

My struggle with Paul began over twenty-five years ago even before I started prayerwalking and intensely studying prayer in the Bible. I got stuck on 1 Thessalonians 5:17: "Pray without ceasing" (NASB). *How?* I wondered. I was a busy mom of four, working full-time as an English teacher. I fell asleep in my cozy chair in the morning trying to pray and nodded off face down in my Bible in bed at night. But Paul's admonition wouldn't leave me. He, too, was on the move constantly.

Someone suggested I read *The Practice of the Presence of God* by Brother Lawrence, the seventeenth-century monastery cook in Paris, who wrote that when he began any task, he would say this childlike prayer:

"O God, since Thou art with me, and it is Thy will that I must now apply myself to these outward duties, I beseech Thee, assist me with Thy grace that I may continue in Thy presence. To this end, O Lord, be with me in this my work, accept the labor of my hands, and dwell within my heart with all Thy fullness."[1]

Then Brother Lawrence wrote that he would continue familiar conversation as he worked, offering up his small acts of service and asking God to help him. However, I had a hard time identifying with Brother Lawrence. Like him, I cooked and washed dishes, but I also did all the grocery shopping and laundry, mowed the lawns, worked a full-time job as an English teacher, graded papers well into the night, toted the kids around to athletics and music practices, took them to doctor appointments, performed extra-duty assignments after hours at school, provided all our school's academic advisement, and volunteered at church—which was another long list. My praying life was on the go, not one just gazing out a kitchen window.

But still I was left with Paul's words: *pray without ceasing*. For an intensive yearlong period I studied other classic writers on prayer—Andrew Murray, Madame Guyon, Teresa of Ávila, Charles Spurgeon, E. M. Bounds, and others—to find the secrets behind how they could pray without ceasing. I wrote a book about my discoveries some years later.[2] What I began to understand was I do not have to sit in a chair or work silently in a kitchen to have a praying life. Just like Paul, I can pray on the go—focused on whatever God puts within my eyesight as he gives me insight.

## Paul's Natural Praying Style

Paul's praying personality comes out definitively in his writings. He responded quickly to directives from Jesus and the Holy Spirit. When the Lord said, "Saul, Saul, why do you persecute me?" and told him to go to Damascus, Paul went (Acts 9:3–9). When the Holy Spirit told him and Barnabas to head out from Antioch, they went. We don't read of an objection or argument such as what God heard from Moses or Gideon.

Prayer was a priority for Paul, and he modeled it for others. D. A. Carson writes:

> One of the remarkable characteristics of Paul's prayers is the large proportion of space devoted to praying for others. Of course, one can find Paul offering simple praise to God and imagine Paul praying for himself. . . . But Paul's prayers . . . are outstanding for the large part intercession for others and thanksgiving for others play in them.[3]

With his own or others' commissionings he prayed and fasted (Acts 13:2–3; 14:23). When Paul left Ephesus, he and the disciples there knelt and prayed, as was true when he left Tyre for Jerusalem (Acts 20:36; 21:5). When Paul was escorted to Rome via ship, and the sea tossed it in a severe storm, he gave thanks to God for their last onboard meal together (Acts 27:35). When Christian believers greeted him in Rome, where he would remain under house arrest, he thanked God for them (Acts 28:15). Prayer was a straightforward, natural part of his response in workings with other people.

We see a results-oriented Paul in his letters. Just as he was straightforward about his discipleship and correction of churches and individuals, so also was his advocacy in prayer for them. Nearly every single letter begins and ends with a benediction. The word *benediction* means "good" (bene-) and "say" (-diction). So this form of prayer is a declaration or announcement of a blessing. The initial benediction is standard from letter to letter, such as this one from Romans 1:7: "Grace and peace to you from God our Father and from the Lord Jesus Christ." This introductory blessing repeats nearly word for word from one letter to another.

To the recipients Paul modeled Jesus, who also prayed blessings over children and who instructed the disciples to bless homes as they entered. While Paul had a results-oriented, achieving, and strong personality—for the sake of the Lord and his kingdom, of course— this kind of introductory prayer may have tempered any criticism that typically followed in his letters, as he often wrote to correct a problem of theology and/or practice.

But such an approach to a letter was not merely perfunctory in nature. It's apparent that Paul prayed faithfully for the people in the churches he planted, also situated in Corinth, Galatia, Ephesus, Philippi, Colossae, and Thessalonica. He often referred to his intercessions for them:

- "Constantly I remember you in my prayers at all times; and I pray that now at last by God's will the way may be opened for me to come to you." (Rom. 1:9–10)
- "I always thank my God for you because of his grace given you in Christ Jesus." (1 Cor. 1:4)
- "For this reason, ever since I heard about your faith in the Lord Jesus and your love for all God's people, I have not stopped giving thanks for you, remembering you in my prayers." (Eph. 1:15–16, written from prison)
- "I thank my God every time I remember you." (Phil. 1:3, written from prison)
- "For this reason, since the day we heard about you, we have not stopped praying for you." (Col. 1:9, written from prison)
- "And we also thank God continually because, when you received the word of God, which you heard from us, you accepted it not as a human word, but as it actually is, the word of God, which is indeed at work in you who believe." (1 Thess. 2:13)

D. A. Carson calls these *prayer reports*—a summary of how Paul (and his associates) prayed.[4] Even while Paul was somewhere else—such as in prison for three of the above remarks—he was praying for those elsewhere. That shows compassion and leadership. A leader not only prays behind the scenes but also takes initiative to demonstrate to others the importance of a praying lifestyle.

## Problem-Solving Focus

Additionally, Paul taught subtly about how to pray as a problem-solving discipline. He wrote, "We do not know what we ought to pray for, but the Spirit himself intercedes for us through wordless groans" (Rom. 8:26). Even Paul didn't always know what to do or how to pray. He showed that when we have a burden, we should lift it in prayer: "Brothers and sisters, my heart's desire and prayer to God for the Israelites is that they may be saved" (Rom. 10:1). Paul also taught the Corinthians that a season of focused prayer without relational distraction is sometimes needed: "Do not deprive each other except perhaps by mutual consent and for a time, so that you may devote yourselves to prayer" (1 Cor. 7:5). And he expected churches to intercede for him in his own struggles. We see this when he wrote, "On him we have set our hope that he will continue to deliver us, as you help us by your prayers" (2 Cor. 1:10–11). Strength is truly shown when strong personalities ask for prayer for themselves.

Teachings about how to function prayerfully within the community of faith are also evidenced in Paul's letters, which reminded his readers others were praying for them. To the Corinthians he wrote that others would pray for them because of their generosity (2 Cor. 9:14). To the Colossians Paul said Epaphras was always "wrestling in prayer" for them—for their spiritual maturity (Col. 4:12). And to the Thessalonians he wrote that he, Silas, and Timothy were constantly praying for them, that they would be worthy of God's calling on their lives, that God would fulfill his purpose through them, and that Jesus would be glorified (2 Thess. 1:11–12). We see a sense of expectancy in Paul's comments, reflecting that he believed prayer would affect the lives of believers.

Each personality type—no matter what assessment method you prefer—has strengths and weaknesses. As we mature in our faith, the weaknesses gradually become less dominant. Paul's characteristics could have been controlling and bossy. Formerly a fanatical persecutor of Christians, he could have created drama. Instead, we see that prayer was a priority for him, and the content of his prayers was focused on others' well-being. Here are some examples from the letter to the Ephesians of what he prayed for them (Eph. 1:17–19):

- The spirit of wisdom and revelation, to know God better
- Enlightened eyes of the heart
- The hope to which God called them
- The riches of God's glorious inheritance
- God's incomparably great power

In other words, Paul prayed for the greatest possible favor for the believers. A strong-minded personality can be competitive, but Paul's prayers show he simply wanted God's best for them. That's a mark of an intercessor, someone who is outwardly focused.

I experienced a shift in prayer focus when I started prayerwalking twenty-five years ago. I prayed for my own needs when I started walking for my health and checking items off my mental prayer list. When God opened my eyes to the needs of others, I was suddenly flooded with the massive concerns around me. Small-town businesses barely surviving. The largest industry folding when the lumber mill shut down and our town shrunk by a third. Hurting marriages (you hear arguments when you regularly walk). Substance and alcohol abuse, as well as areas of blight and seeming apathy.

I began to sense an ownership or responsibility in prayer for my community. It needed me to pray. The people needed my faithfulness. Those thoughts were confirmed one evening when I read Haggai 2:23: "'On that day,' declares the LORD Almighty, 'I will take you, my servant Zerubbabel son of Shealtiel,' declares the LORD, 'and I will make you like my signet ring, for I have chosen you,' declares the LORD Almighty." A burden to intercede for the thousand folks in my town struck me deeply—especially the thought that God had chosen me to be his representative in prayer. A king used a signet ring to stamp his mark on approved edicts that would govern people's lives and behaviors. The mark was the king's authority. I sensed a weight to lift up the needs of the people around me—needs they themselves may not have known.

We see that sense of responsibility in Paul. There were others who were spreading the good news to the non-Jewish world in the Mediterranean area—Silas, John Mark, Timothy, and some whose names we may never know. But we can see this signet-ring kind of representation in Paul's prayers for others. He owned the burden to intercede. People came to the faith because of his preaching and teaching, but he did not forget them. He remembered them in prayer.

You may have that problem-solving tendency if your thoughts immediately go to fixing someone's problem when you hear them talking. If so, you may have a calling to pray for your community. Perhaps your town needs you to pray for the various problems that seem to scream at you when you walk or drive by. And perhaps you could experience the unspeakable joy of answered prayers when you notice the very changes for which you prayed.

## Paul, the Praying Pastor

I have not yet touched on Paul's prayers in his pastoral letters to Timothy, Titus, and Philemon (and others with him). His benedictions in those letters were also seasoned with affectionate salutations before he expressed the benedictory prayer:

- "To Timothy, my true son in the faith . . ." (1 Tim. 1:2)
- "To Titus, my true son in our common faith . . ." (Titus 1:4)

- "To Philemon our dear friend and fellow worker—also to Apphia our sister and Archippus our fellow soldier—and to the church that meets in your home . . ." (Philem. 1–2)

There's a funny thing that can happen with prayer: you begin to love the people for whom you pray, even if you don't know them, and even if you had previously not liked them at all. I'm not making the argument that Paul did not have regard for these people before writing his letters, but with his words he again models to those with whom he has ministered and discipled how they also can hold others up in prayerful expressions. As he did with the letters to the churches, Paul closed with a benediction, typically asking that grace be with each one. He prayed for their best in a hopeful, expectant manner.

Intercession is certainly a high calling—considered by many to be a spiritual gift—but it also is a mark of those mature in the faith. D. A. Carson speaks to this:

> If we follow Paul's example, then, we will never overlook the monumental importance of praying for *others*. Prayer will never descend to the level where it is nothing more than a retreat house in which we find strength for ourselves, whether through the celebration of praise or through a mystic communion with God or through the relief of casting our cares upon the Almighty. Prayer may embrace all these elements, and more, but if we learn to pray with Paul, we will learn to pray for others. We will see it is part of our job to approach God with thanksgiving for others and with intercessions for others. In short, our praying will be shaped by our profound desire to seek what is best for the people of God.[5]

In contrast, while James exhorted the recipients of his letter to pray, he did not indicate that he did so himself. The same is true for Peter

(1 Pet. 4:7), other than his benedictions at the beginnings and end-
ings of his two letters. Only one of John's letters has a teaching about
asking God for anything according to his will (1 John 5:14–15). Paul,
on the other hand, clearly held prayer of high importance. He began
his letters with prayer. He ended them with prayer. He often reported
about his prayers for the recipients of the letters. And he offered prayers
in the body of the letter and exhorted the people to pray as well.

I believe we are all called to intercede. It develops compassion in us, as
well as humility and gratefulness. I should notice others' needs. I should
care about their sufferings. And I should take the time daily to pray for
those I love, as well as those who need God's provision, care, and grace.

## ──────── PRAYER POINTERS ────────

- Respond quickly to the Spirit's nudges. Pray and obey with responsive action.
- Intercede for those you meet during your day and those with
  whom you correspond, message, or text. Everywhere you go,
  there is a need for prayer.
- Fill dead headspace with prayer: pray during commutes, household tasks, exercise.
- Make fasting part of your practice when praying for spiritual
  breakthrough in others' lives or in your own.
- Rejoice in the Lord always: for example, "Thank you, Lord, for
  this flat tire today."
- Give thanks in all circumstances.
- Be expectant in prayer. Pray big prayers when encountering challenges and anticipate that God will answer with his perfect will.
- Pray in response to needs you see on social media. Close your
  eyes for a minute and focus on those folks, lifting their needs in
  prayer.
- Respond to temptation with prayer, asking God to deliver you
  from its pull.

## DISCUSSION QUESTIONS

1. Why do you think the author called Paul the "on-the-run intercessor"?

2. How do you respond to Paul's admonition in 1 Thessalonians 5:17 (NASB): "Pray without ceasing"?

3. How was prayer Paul's response as he dealt with many of those he mentored in the faith?

4. How did Paul model prayer as a problem-solving response? What are some of his examples of that kind of prayer?

5. How could our prayers help pastor others?

6. How does intercession help us grow in our faith?

7. Do any of the Prayer Pointers appeal to you? Which ones and why?

# PART TWO

## Personality Types

*Chapter 8*

# The Classic Temperaments

I STRUGGLED A LOT AS a young adult. I got frustrated easily, complained a lot, and blew off steam at my husband and our kids. I also felt depressed and hopeless often. I knew something was wrong with me. The clincher was when I was in a couples' Bible study in our church and this question was asked: *Are you content?* Of the twelve married couples in that room—men and women—I was the only person who said she was not content. The thought that something was wrong with me continued for the next half dozen years or so.

Perhaps you've sensed this kind of inner tension. Two kinds of reading helped me understand myself better: reading the Bible more consistently and reading about the differences in personality—in particular, books on the four classic temperaments, which physician and philosopher Hippocrates (c. 460–370 BC) first identified. After reading a half dozen books released by Christian publishers on the subject, I was able to understand my God-given personality and see my personal strengths and weaknesses more clearly. Reading temperament discussions of biblical characters also helped me understand them better (impulsive Peter, resistant Moses, emotional David). Studying the temperaments was freeing but also challenging. I wanted to live into my strengths and leave my weaknesses in the dust.

In fact, one day I was visiting with an older woman when I realized she had the same temperament as I did but was manifesting most of the negative characteristics and not the strengths. *I could be like her in another twenty-five years.* That thought shook me up, and I prayed right then that God would help me grow into my strengths and away from my weaknesses. Those studies, combined with that moment, were a pivotal point in my life—one that eventually directed me to submit my life to Christ's lordship and God's calling on my life. I doubt I would now be a writer without having studied the temperaments.

Another Greek, Aristotle, said, "Knowing yourself is the beginning of all wisdom." People of faith understand that knowing *God* is the starting place for acquiring wisdom. However, knowing yourself can help you understand your good points and your flaws and become a better person. And understanding the temperaments also helps you understand others and the way they think and respond. At the heart of growing in spiritual maturity is prayer, but understanding your personality certainly can help you deepen your prayer life.

There are four classic temperaments: sanguine, choleric, melancholy, and phlegmatic. The outgoing sanguine is enthusiastic and people-oriented but may have a hard time sticking to a routine. The choleric is goal-driven leadership material but can be impatient and find it hard to relax. The reserved melancholy is a deep thinker and feeler, but perfectionism and depression can be derailing. The consistent phlegmatic is slow to commit to a practice but isn't easily ruffled. They're all different in behavior, so each may be suited to a different kind of prayer style.

In this chapter we'll examine each temperament with its personal characteristics. Most discussions of temperament have lists of positive characteristics and negative ones. Instead, to get a more well-rounded picture of each personality, we will answer the following questions for each:

- What is their overall personality and how do they present themselves to the world?
- What is their outlook toward the world around them?
- How do they view and approach work?
- How do they approach their spiritual life?

It may be possible to see yourself in more than one of these four temperaments. Chances are, however, that one is the dominant with a secondary one also striking home.

## The Sanguine

The word *sanguine* comes from the Latin *sanguineus*, which means "blood" or "blood red"—and the connection to the temperament is the lifeblood or enthusiastic element we see in those with this personality. The sanguine is a socially comfortable, outgoing person who thrives in the company of others. She brings a party to the room with her animated, playful behavior, wide smile, and pleasant disposition. Talkative and loud, she loves telling stories, laughing a lot, and having long conversations, and if those conversations are in person, that's better than on the phone. In fact, when she is surrounded by people, she's at her happiest and does not mind being the center of attention. She makes friends easily and loves participating in group sports and activities with others. Emotionally centered, she can have mood swings, but is typically cheerful, interested, talkative, and sincere. She will give you her honest opinion—but it may be spontaneously expressed without a lot of forethought.

### Outlook

The sanguine sees the positive side of a situation and has a high level of expectancy that life will be good each day—that even if there are problems, they will have a good outcome. This innocent and perhaps even naïve approach to life is refreshing to others, who are drawn to this personality—one that lives in the perspective that life should be enjoyable and fun. Feelings are all-important to the sanguine, who needs to be happy and fun, so when things do not work out, she can take an emotional dive. Typically, though, it would not last long, because the sanguine doesn't want to miss out on anything.

## Work

Every working team needs a sanguine who will be the charismatic, visionary influencer coming up with new ideas and inspiring others to grab hold of the vision and "go for it." She's good at recruiting others to join the team but is not necessarily good at planning the details, organizing tasks, or remembering to do them. Time can get away from her, and she's often late. The sanguine is decisive and enthusiastic about a new program but sometimes decisions have not been thoroughly thought through, so enthusiasm for a long-term project can peter out. The sanguine would be wise not to jump right into new projects immediately but instead incorporate a practice of putting some space between the original thought and the decision to move forward. Sanguines might find it more realistic to have someone break a larger goal down into step-by-step tasks with definitive deadlines for each, along with accountability from the team or employer. This temperament might work best as a supervisor because she would be an encourager to others carrying out the specific tasks. On the flip side, her love for conversation can pull others off task.

## Spiritual Life

The sanguine might have the toughest of the four temperaments for maintaining her spiritual disciplines. She will love attending church but may find it hard to get there on time. The sanguine will also enthusiastically and sincerely sign up for in-person Bible studies or small groups but may fall behind in the actual studies or forget to attend.

Personal Bible reading and prayer times may also be hit or miss—with eager start-ups of new devotional books or reading plans, as well as different prayer strategies. Perhaps she'll even get her friends to start with her—but then fall behind and give up as her overcommitted schedule begins to drive her behavior. Essentially, she needs a praying practice that has flexibility and spontaneity.

─────────── **PRAYER POINTERS** ───────────

- Make it a practice to pray with people, so it is something you look forward to.
- Respond to others with prayer. They confide easily in you, so say, "Let me pray for you right now."
- Make prayer fun. If you have a family, let each person take a minute to pray for something in a family circle or in the car. Let the last person who prays choose the next person.
- Put worship music on at home and pray as you sing. Encourage others to join in.
- Pray out loud in the car when you're by yourself. Your music will keep you company!

## The Choleric

The word *choleric* comes from the Greek word *cholerikós*, which means "bile" or "bilious"—intimating that this temperament is prone to being irritable or unpleasant. As a personality the choleric is confident and determined. In social settings he's interested in goals rather than people, so while extroverted in nature, he is ready to put the event behind him and move on to the next objective. He has a hard time relaxing, and vacations might be filled with various activities as opposed to reading and conversation. The choleric prefers having his hands busy doing something productive while conversing, as he values action more than conversation. Problem-solving comes naturally, and he relishes production and achievement. Cholerics want to be in control—whether that's choosing a restaurant or the best route to a destination. When he is not in control, he can feel frustrated and even angry.

## Outlook
Cholerics are serious in nature and positive in regard to their own abilities, but they can be negative and critical toward other people and what they bring to the table. They are willing to take risks because with their driven nature they have experienced success in the past. Change is not threatening to them—just a series of new challenges to meet and conquer.

## Work
The choleric is a workaholic who does not require a lot of sleep. He's a natural manager who can assess situations clearly and make decisions that benefit an organization. If the organization has an overall objective, he will own that and work toward achieving it. He loves a challenge—perhaps even a problem others haven't been able to solve. Unfinished tasks will drive him crazy, and he'll work until the job is done. Cholerics don't work well in a group because they grow impatient with coming to a consensus about how to proceed and prefer doing the assignment on their own—because they believe they know how to do it right. Results drive them, and they're confident they know how to produce those results. They are detail-oriented and good planners. While the job will get done, their personality tendencies can have some negative effects: they can alienate others who don't feel valued, and they can get overwhelmed because they've taken on more than was meant for them to do. Others can take offense from cholerics' tendency to take over and discount others' contributions, so those with this temperament need to learn how to delegate, to trust others, and to

connect on a personal level—expressing their appreciation for qualities of others in their lives.

### Spiritual Life

Cholerics do not like waiting, so giving up control to a God who doesn't always respond to prayers with a quick turnaround can frustrate this temperament. The choleric might find his prayers are a list of objectives: *Heal Tom. Get me that job, God. Let me get through that green light.* He might have a hard time sitting still in prayerful reflection, waiting for God's direction and spending time in praise and thanksgiving. However, cholerics accomplish their daily devotional and Bible reading. Those are tasks they can work through as part of their daily to-do checklist. Their praying life needs to help them have a sense of achievement and forward movement, as opposed to extended, sit-in-place quiet time.

─────── PRAYER POINTERS ───────

- Multitask your prayer life. Pray while you walk or work out.
- Take your problems and to-do lists to the Problem Solver in prayer first. Ask God for his direction.
- Consider starting a prayer network because leadership comes naturally for you.
- Know that God hears your short prayers—even "Help!"
- Pray through the Bible as you read its pages.
- Pray right when you sense a need and turn it over to God.

## The Melancholy

The word *melancholy* comes from the Greek *melancholia*, which means "black bile"—referring to the side of this personality that can lean toward sadness or even depression. This state can result from having very high, perfectionistic standards that are hard to achieve; thus, those who are melancholy may often be hard on themselves because they sense they are falling short of those standards. They are thoughtful, faithful, and persistent, and they are detail-oriented and creative in the arts and in problem-solving. Melancholies are sensitive in nature and can take any criticism—direct or simply inferred—to heart. Highly introverted, they need time alone, especially after being in environments with lots of stimuli. They are serious in nature and reflective—often thinking deeply and offering insightful ideas they have processed.

### Outlook

Melancholies have an idealistic view of life—with high standards for others as well as themselves. Because people are flawed, melancholies often have a pessimistic perspective, anticipating problems and thinking that the worst will happen. With a deep compassion for the world, they bear the hurts of others and take on social causes. Those of the melancholy temperament look for, think about, and process meaning from life's situations, and their creative art may be expressed in music, visual arts, and literature.

### Work

If you want something done with meticulous detail, hire a melancholy. They do exhaustive research to come up with the best strategy, create a detailed plan, and work slowly and carefully until the project is completed to perfection. They can also procrastinate for fear of not being able to complete the job well; sometimes deadlines might not be met because of initial resistance about getting it done exactly right, but they will eventually work tirelessly toward its completion. Melancholies are worker bees who enjoy organizing systems, analyzing research and data, and finding creative solutions to problems. And they need lots of encouragement in work and volunteer situations because they are their own worst critics and may be convinced their work isn't worthy.

### Spiritual Life

The melancholy person loves spiritual disciplines that allow her to get away from the world. She will create a quiet, cozy spot for devotional time and use scheduled systems to read the Word and incorporate prayer times into her life. She's unsure of herself and her worth in God's sight, so she sensitively reacts to biblical and devotional readings and thinks deeply about their meaning and application for her own life. Because this person may have creative gifts, she may find artistic ways to express her faith through worship or art forms. Doing these practices methodically is an important value to a melancholy, but she will find a way to make that daily practice special.

—————— PRAYER POINTERS ——————

- Find a system to keep track of your prayers—such as a binder or spiral notebook or even a file you keep on your computer—because you are a detail-oriented person.
- Use a journal to write out your prayers.
- Pray as you create artwork.
- Prayerfully journal through the Bible as you read. Draw out a focus Scripture verse using colored pencils or markers. Pray as you create a picture in the margin of your Bible that reflects thoughts behind something you read.
- Don't worry about getting your prayer life perfect. Enjoy the time with the Lord—whenever or whatever that looks like.

## The Phlegmatic

The word *phlegmatic* comes from the Greek *phlegmatikós*, which means "pertaining to phlegm"—referring to the slow or sluggish nature of those with this temperament. The phlegmatics are service-oriented folks who love to help. They demonstrate a mellow, relaxed, easygoing personality that is not emotionally reactive. In a crisis they are calm and collected and avoid those who continually create emotional havoc.

## Outlook

The phlegmatic values peace and strives to create unity. Possessing a low-key nature, he has a positive outlook and seeks out and is easily contented with a well-balanced lifestyle. While introverted, this person is outward-focused—friendly, patient, and agreeable—and seeks to help others rather than focusing on his own needs. His main goal is to live in peace with those around him and thus, will take on the role of peacemaker or moderator.

## Work

Phlegmatics work well in service-oriented jobs, such as health care or hospitality. While it may take a long time for a phlegmatic to start and then gain momentum on a project, he will then thrive in routines with clearly expressed expectations. While he is slow to make decisions, those decisions will be carefully thought through. He is compliant and faithful but sometimes there may be an issue with the level of intensity toward a project because his momentum may fade. A team or partner approach is successful with external accountability. He doesn't need attention or accolades and is eager to help. The phlegmatic desires to stay in sync with others, and he is most successful when projects are broken down into systematic tasks with regular meetings. A supervisor will find that those with the phlegmatic temperament are steady and supportive of the overall mission.

## Spiritual Life

Because of the phlegmatic's relaxed nature, he may struggle to get his own spiritual practices into place. If part of a small group with regular meetings and accountability, he will mature in the faith slowly but steadily. His greatest spiritual need may be God's infilling, because from day to day the phlegmatic has been giving to and serving others without regard to his own deficits. He will thrive spiritually with a daily routine.

―――――――――― PRAYER POINTERS ――――――――

- Make prayer easy for you but also make it a priority. When are you the freshest during the day? Pray then. You desire balance in your life: prayer will help you find that sweet spot.
- Don't worry about getting all the words right. God knows your heart—just speak what's on it.
- Find a quiet place that becomes your routine place to pray.
- Remove distractions like your cell phone or computer in your prayer spot.
- Consider joining prayer teams and networks—you have a lot to offer with your desire to serve and help.

―――――――――― DISCUSSION QUESTIONS ――――――――

1. How would you summarize the sanguine personality? the choleric personality? the melancholy personality? the phlegmatic personality?
2. Do you see yourself mostly in one or two of those temperaments? Which ones and why?
3. What is your strongest personality characteristic? And a point of weakness?
4. Do any of the Prayer Pointers appeal to you? Which ones and why?

*Chapter 9*

# The Modern Personalities

WHEN I TAUGHT HIGH SCHOOL students, I also served as our small school's only academic advisor. One important field trip I arranged took juniors and seniors to a college fair. Besides having the opportunity to talk to college and tech school representatives, my juniors and seniors participated in engaging workshops with the college students. One of those was a personality workshop that used animal figures to represent the various personalities, like this:

- The authoritative Lion (choleric)
- The enthusiastic Otter (sanguine)
- The sensitive Golden Retriever (phlegmatic)
- The orderly Beaver (melancholy)[1]

The students quickly related to those animals, although they often misinterpreted what their personalities were. There sure were a lot of "sensitive Golden Retrievers" on the way home, but they were all barking a lot—some sweetly, some not so much—instead of just smiling and wagging their tails.

At the end of one of those trips one of my students said, "Mrs. McHenry, do we still have to turn in that essay tomorrow?"

"Yes, you do."

"Mrs. McHenry," she said with a groan, "you're such a bear."

"No," I said, "I am a lion, and watch me roar."

Over the last century people have created many other kinds of personality assessments that echo the temperaments framework Hippocrates created. In 1940 Walter Clark took the personality theories of William Moulton Marston (who did not want to create an assessment) and created the DISC assessment, which stands for Dominance, Influence, Steadiness, and Compliance. (Did you notice the correlation with the choleric, sanguine, phlegmatic, and melancholy temperaments?) Family Christian counselor Gary Smalley created the personality assessment using the animal figures (found in Chapter 10 of his 1997 book *Making Love Last Forever*).

An increasingly popular, newer system is called LINKED®, with the personalities identified as the Mobilizer (choleric), Socializer (sanguine), Stabilizer (phlegmatic), and Organizer (melancholy)—created in 2018 by Linda Gilden and Linda Goldfarb. I particularly appreciate this last approach because it makes identification simple with its series of quick guides for parents, educators, writers, leaders, and teens. As a self-professed Mobilizer, I appreciate this succinct approach instead of having to wade through hundreds of pages of psychological data and analysis, because Mobilizers like to "get things done fast."

## Carl Jung's Studies

Then there are the systems built from Swiss psychologist Carl Jung's studies and his 1923 book *Personality Types*. Called the father of analytical psychology, Jung said there are four main functions of consciousness. Two are perceiving or nonrational functions: sensation (use of the senses to perceive something) and intuition (use of instinct or hunch to perceive something). And the two other consciousness functions are thinking (using reason) and feeling (relying upon feeling). Two additional factors modify these four functions, Jung said:

extraversion (orientation toward the outer world) and introversion (orientation toward one's own mental world). From the mix of these he identified eight personality types:

- The extroverted sensation (ES) type values intense realism.
- The introverted sensation (NS) type is influenced by mood and experience.
- The extroverted intuition (EN) type looks for new experiences, change, and possibilities.
- The introverted intuition (IN) type chases unconscious possibilities without creating personal connection.
- The extroverted thinking (ET) type builds thinking from education or tradition.
- The introverted thinking (IT) type seeks to understand through culture.
- The extroverted feeling (EF) type expresses feelings properly.
- The introverted feeling (IF) type shies away from others or change.

Note that Jung's type system uses just *two* indicators: one of the first four indicators—sensation, intuition, thinking, or feeling—plus either introversion or extraversion.

The Jungian ideas may sound complicated and amorphous, but we can boil them down to three questions:

- Do you tend to understand something by rational data you take in with your five senses (sensation) or do you just rely on your good instincts (intuition)?
- Do you primarily use reason (thinking) or feeling to make decisions?
- Are you extroverted (gain energy from being around people) or introverted (prefer to be by yourself)?

I struggled to understand these differences until I thought of a couple of examples.

First, let's look at the difference between *sensation* and *intuition*. I recently put together some patio furniture I ordered, but I did not read or even look at the directions. I typically just follow my hunches and best guesses, which shows I tend to understand through intuition. My husband is the opposite. For our first trip to Hawaii, he bought a new camera, and on the five-hour flight there he read the entire manual from cover to cover. He must read and see to understand. I just follow my gut. Intuitives will just know when to pray. They may wake up in the middle of the night and have a feeling they should pray for someone. Sensers need to see or hear about a need for prayer.

Next, let's examine the difference between *thinking* and *feeling*. As an academic advisor, I guided students through the college, financial aid, and scholarship application processes. I also advised that students visit each campus, if possible, before making a final decision. Over the years I noticed that some students based their decisions on the black and white: pros-and-cons lists and financial aid offers. These young people would have a thinking-based personality (or their parents did!). In contrast, feelers might simply visit a college campus and just *know* it's right for them. Both personalities might find themselves living college life happily ever after, and both might also find they want to make a change down the road—thinkers because their data was skewed and feelers because their impressions were false. Thinking pray-ers might keep lists; feeling pray-ers might wait for inspiration to strike. Both could be praying for the very same thing.

Lastly, and related to this Jungian thought, an illustration from Simon Sinek helps explain the difference between the *extrovert* and the *introvert*. He calls this the coin theory. Extroverts start their day with zero coins but gain coins throughout their day as they interact with others; they fill their emotional pockets with social interaction. Introverts start their day with five coins, and as their day proceeds in various interactions with others, they lose a coin with each one. By the end of their day, their emotional pockets might easily be empty . . . if not in a deficit situation.[2] The extrovert gains energy from social interaction; the introvert loses energy from it. Extroverts will look forward to praying with groups of people; introverts will want to run to their private prayer closets away from the madding crowd.

Numerous articles I've read point to the problematic issue that personality tests can be unreliable. People can take the same test several times and come up with different answers each time. There's also the issue that we do not always see ourselves in the correct light. As we take these assessments, we might choose the answers we want to be true, rather than respond with the way we actually are. If I'd taken a poll of my students on the return trip of one of my college fair field trips, almost the whole busload would have said they were extroverted. They wanted to be perceived as fun and lively, when the truth often was many were eventually dead asleep on the bus ride home because they were in an energy deficit from all the interaction they had just experienced talking to college reps and others. Because I still struggle with answering those quizzes and because I've seen others assess themselves incorrectly, I have tried to get to the bottom-line questions that underlie those assessments.

## PRAYER POINTERS

- For extroverts, consider prayer a natural part of your gatherings with others, even with just a simple, "Let's pray about that right now." Your challenge will always be to step away from the crowd to pray because of a sense that you'll miss something, but there's much value in getting time alone too.
- For introverts, find that quiet place where you can get away from the noise and distractions from others and media. Your challenge will be participating with others in prayer because that's not your comfort zone. However, you can simply listen and pray silently.

- For sensers (those who rely upon reality as opposed to instinct), pray for that which you see and experience. Learn to trust God for intuitive ideas—and pray for them too, as they arise.
- For intuitives (those who rely upon instinct over what is seen and perceived by the senses), pray when those gut instincts or hunches arise. When God brings a person to mind, pray. When you think something isn't quite right, pray. As a stretching point, learn to value what your natural senses are showing you and pray for the reality of what you experience.
- For thinkers (those who rely on reason over feeling), decide how you will pray. Create a pattern for prayer that works with your schedule and lifestyle.
- For feelers (those who rely on feelings over reason), pray as God leads you—in the moment, on the go, wherever you are, whatever you feel in the situation.

## Myers-Briggs Type Indicator

In 1917 Katherine Cook Briggs began studying personality, creating four temperament types: meditative (or thoughtful), spontaneous, executive, and social. Then when she studied Jung's work, she and her daughter, Isabel Briggs Myers, created their own personality assessment during the time period of World War II—eventually called the Myers-Briggs Type Indicator (MBTI), which has been widely used in business and education settings.[3]

As I perceive it, the MBTI test is focused on four questions:

- Are you introverted or extroverted? Does being with people deplete your energy (introverted I) or give you energy (extroverted E)?
- How do you prefer to receive information? Do you focus on reality, details, and specifics (the sensing S)? Or do you like to dream, look for the big picture, and enjoy ideas for their own sake (the intuition N)?

- How do you prefer to make decisions? Do you use logical arguments (the thinking T) or do you consider values, empathy, and pleasing behavior (the feeling F)?
- How do you prefer to live your life? Do you like matters settled and prefer following rules, schedules, and deadlines (the judging J)? Or do you prefer keeping your options open, improvising as you go along (the perceiving P)?[4]

The first three questions are pretty much the same ones Jung asked, while Myers and Briggs added the last one. The other change is that the MBTI uses four indicators—like INFJ, for example—to indicate a personality type rather than just the two that Jung used, resulting in sixteen different personalities that the MBTI identifies.

These various kinds of thinking, feeling, and behaving may lead to specific kinds of natural prayer styles. For example, the INFJ (introverted-intuition-feeling-judging type) is a natural counselor and may find she prays intuitively as she spends time with people and feels the struggles they're going through. The ESFP (extroverted-sensing-feeling-perceiving type) might be the one to enthusiastically start a weekly prayer service at her church but will need the INTJ (introverted-intuitive-thinking-judging type) to organize and carry out all the details. Each of the sixteen personalities could have a praying style that meshes in a simpatico fashion.

## PRAYER POINTERS

- For those who lean toward judging, consider setting up a plan for how you'll approach prayer, as you prefer rules and schedules.
- For those who lean toward perceiving, integrate prayer into your lifestyle as you go through your day because improvisation comes more naturally to you.
- Note: See also the Prayer Pointers for the Jungian personality

characteristics, which correspond to the first three Myers-Briggs categories.

## Keirsey Temperament Sorter

After studying the Myers-Briggs Type Indicator, David Keirsey created his own personality assessment called the Keirsey Temperament Sorter (KTS). This mechanism was made popular by his books *Please Understand Me: Character and Temperament Types* (1978) and *Please Understand Me II: Temperament, Character, Intelligence* (1998, co-authored with Marilyn Bates). He, however, took Hippocrates's four temperaments—sanguine, choleric, phlegmatic, and melancholy—and renamed them after the Greek gods Dionysus, Apollo, Prometheus, and Epimetheus. Understanding that these gods had negative characteristics, he chose to focus on positive aspects instead—calling the four major personality categories Artisan, Idealist, Rational, and Guardian. Instead of focusing on how people think or feel, as does the Myers-Briggs, the KTS focuses its test questions on how people behave—something others can perhaps objectify more easily.

Each of those four temperaments is then broken down into two roles, each of which is then broken down into two variants, like this:[5]

| Temperament | Role | Role Variant |
|---|---|---|
| Idealist | Mentor | Teacher |
| | | Counselor |
| | Advocate | Champion |
| | | Healer |
| Rational | Coordinator | Fieldmarshal |
| | | Mastermind |
| | Engineer | Inventor |
| | | Architect |

| Guardian | Administrator | Supervisor |
| --- | --- | --- |
| | | Inspector |
| | Conservator | Provider |
| | | Protector |
| Artisan | Operator | Promoter |
| | | Crafter |
| | Entertainer | Performer |
| | | Composer |

Notice that each of the roles is positive in nature. Who wouldn't want to be perceived as a provider or architect? While Keirsey said he didn't base his personalities on those of Myers-Briggs, I find it a bit amusing that even before taking the Keirsey assessment (which is in each of his books), I could immediately point to Mastermind on the chart, which is identified as INTJ (introverted-intuition-thinking-judging)—the same as I tend to score on the MBTI. Again, it is helpful to see these laid out in terms of roles, because we can gravitate more easily to one that naturally represents how we behave societally.

These roles, too, can help us understand how we are drawn to one kind of praying style over another. For example, the Mastermind pray-er goes to God in prayer because he is the ultimate Problem Solver, as I frequently refer to the Lord. I might have moments of skepticism in my faith, but honestly, I frequently pray, "Lord, I believe; help my unbelief!" (Mark 9:24 NKJV). I trust God, because I have read his Word, know his promises, and have seen him work out the impossible in my life and that of my family members. And I keep praying for God to move because I am strong-willed and want to see answers to my prayers. The pragmatic side of me, however, will also pray, "Your will be done," because I know God's sovereign plan is best.

Hopefully, you are beginning to see a pattern that while it's beneficial to study the personalities, it's much more important to understand the character of God and his view of who we are. Then we truly know what he would have us do in our prayer closets—whatever they might look like.

## PRAYER POINTERS

- Idealist: Because you are a strong advocate and champion, consider intercession as a prayer strength. You naturally see others and their needs and want to come alongside them to help and see healing in their lives. As you encounter others throughout your day, pray for them when you learn of their needs.
- Rational: See God as your Problem Solver. Although you naturally will want to mastermind and engineer solutions to your own and others' problems, take them to prayer first. See prayer as your first response, rather than as a last resort. Ask God continually for his insight.
- Guardian: Because you are a good manager and supervisor, set up a prayer plan for yourself. Look at your schedule and make a daily appointment with God. Follow through with that just as you would in other aspects of your life. Pray for those folks under your care—they need your prayers as much as the physical help you provide.
- Artisan: Be a champion of prayer. Model it for others. Approach prayer creatively through artistic means, such as poetry, visual art, and music.

## 16 Personalities

The 16 Personalities assessment builds on a Myers-Briggs schema, adding another indicator. Its test is divided into these five personality aspects:

- Mind: How do you interact with your surroundings? If you are sensitive to external stimulation, you are Introverted (I). If you are energized by social interaction, you are Extroverted (E).
- Energy: How do you see the world and process information? If you are a very down-to-earth, practical person, you are Observant (S). If you are more open-minded and imaginative, you are Intuitive (N).
- Nature: How do you cope with emotions and make decisions? If you are a logical processor and focus on the facts, you are Thinking (T). If you are more emotionally based, you are Feeling (F).
- Tactics: How do you approach work, planning, and decision-making? If you are decisive and prefer structure, you are Judging (J). If you are more flexible and prefer improvising in a situation, you are Prospecting (P).
- Identity: How confident are you in your abilities and decisions? If you don't worry much and are self-assured, you are Assertive (A). If you react emotionally to stress and are success-driven and perfectionistic, you are Turbulent (T).[6]

These indicators are then grouped into four letters, plus one extra, which together represent the following:

- Inner layer: Intuitive (N) or Observant (S) + Thinking (T) or Feeling (F)
- Outer layer: Extroverted (E) or Introverted (I) + Judging (J) or Prospecting (P)
- Additional indicator of either Assertive (A) or Turbulent (T)

Then the assessment divides the personalities into four different roles (like occupational tendencies): Analysts, Diplomats, Sentinels, and Explorers. And each of those has four different strategies (ways they work): Confident Individualism, People Mastery, Constant Improvement, and Social Engagement.

The 16 Personalities organization provides not only a free test but also free results, which the great majority of other assessments do not. My results came out like this: INTJ-A/INTJ-T. When I am assertive (which came up as 69 percent), I demonstrate the personality of the Assertive Advocate, someone who is confident and relaxed. When I am turbulent (31 percent), I demonstrate the personality of the Turbulent Advocate—questioning myself and showing sensitivity to stressors.

The test is helpful because it allows you to see percentages with these tendencies. For example, I am mostly (57 percent) Introverted according to this test, which explains why I begin to fade into the wallpaper after prolonged social engagement. I'm fairly even in my spread between Intuitive (55 percent) and Observant (45 percent), so that explains why I like having the facts but often go with my best hunch instead of reading all of the data before making a decision. I trust my hunches. The one indicator that made me laugh was the Judging-Prospecting area; I am 94 percent Judging, which means I'm decisive. But take me to a restaurant, and I can never decide what I want.

The end results are expressed in life roles, some of which sound like the biblical characters we studied earlier. Some of those roles, for example, are Debater, Advocate, Mediator, and Campaigner, which sound much like the praying roles of biblical characters that I identified earlier: Adam, the Questioner; Job, the Thinker; Jacob, the Negotiator; Moses, the Dialoguer; and Gideon, the Sign Requester. Because the 16 Personalities assessment identifies personality types in terms of roles rather than careers or descriptions, it's natural to think about how each personality would instinctively fit into a certain kind of praying style. While I need to know myself well to take the test correctly, it does seem easier to see myself in one or more of those roles.

─────── **PRAYER POINTERS** ───────

- Assertive Identity: Pray big. You have confidence in God and have seen answers to prayer in your life. Continue to lift the weights of the world because others trust the faith you demonstrate. Remember not to take pride in answers to your prayers because it is God who brings about the results.
- Turbulent Identity: Take time and space away from the world to pray for those burdens that you feel deeply—your own and those of others. Don't worry about getting a routine perfect—God will delight in your presence.
- Note: As the 16 Personalities build on the Jungian and Myers-Briggs ideas, also see Prayer Pointers relating to those above.

## StrengthsFinder

My husband is a cattle rancher who's as contented as a cow when he doesn't have to deal with people. He's introverted and focused on getting tasks accomplished. This year God blessed him with an abundant hay crop, so he found that instead of having only enough for his own beef cattle, he could sell a lot of it. That's a nice problem, except that it's challenging meeting the demands of folks who want to come and go at all hours, any day of the week—when he's the only one working on the ranch, with a lot to do.

Enter our oldest, Rebekah, who decided to partner with him in the hay business. She's a people-first kind of person who enjoys interacting with others and whom others immediately connect with, enjoy, and trust. Rebekah has what the CliftonStrengths assessment would call Woo. She has that charisma, that social magnetism that brings energy and spark to relationships, teams, and work environments. People with Woo quickly meet others, break the ice, and turn strangers into friends. She is drawn to people, and people are not only drawn to her but love her.

If you've applied for a job in the last twenty or so years, you might have been asked to take a test called StrengthsFinder—also known as Clifton StrengthsFinder and now, CliftonStrengths. Donald O. Clifton created the assessment that focuses on a person's strengths—not so much personality, but actual skills. He was an American psychologist, researcher, and businessman who founded Selection Research, Inc., which later acquired Gallup Inc., the organization that performs various polls in the United States.[7] Businesses and other organizations have used this assessment to determine if a certain applicant would meet the particular needs of the company, based on how they score on the test.

The test, which I've taken, identifies thirty-four different strengths a person might have, categorized into four different domains, as follows:

| Strategic Thinking | Relationship Building | Influencing | Executing |
|---|---|---|---|
| Analytical | Adaptability | Activator | Achiever |
| Context | Connectedness | Command | Arranger |
| Futuristic | Developer | Communication | Belief |
| Ideation | Empathy | Competition | Consistency |
| Input | Harmony | Maximizer | Deliberative |
| Intellection | Includer | Self-Assurance | Discipline |
| Learner | Individualization | Significance | Focus |
| Strategic | Positivity | Woo | Responsibility |
| | Relator | | Restorative |

My test showed that my top five "themes" are Harmony, Activator, Communication, Input, and Relator. Frankly, while I think I mistook the quiz for the first few questions, I was surprised when I read the descriptions of each, as they seemed to nail my strengths. For example, even though I would not have picked Harmony for one of my strengths, I believe these behaviors are true for me: practical thinker, asks experts, straightforward, sincere, avoids favoritism, good natured, businesslike, focused attention, and measured, consistent progress.

Some of these behaviors could certainly describe my prayer life. I sometimes refer to God as the Problem Solver, and I go to him with problems—others' and my own. My prayers are not long and elaborate; they're succinctly to the point. I am sincere with my prayers, but I typically am not an emotional pray-er. However, those on the prayer team at my church could tell you they occasionally hear emotion in my prayers as we pray together on Sunday mornings for our church and its leadership.

Because the tests we've discussed in this chapter are copyrighted, I cannot share all their personality summaries and details, but you could take any one of them (most, other than 16Personalities.com, require a fee) and find the test results helpful as you seek a praying lifestyle.

## PRAYER POINTERS

- Strategic Thinkers: Think outside the prayer box. You don't have to do prayer the way your family does—especially if those practices don't feel effective for your lifestyle. However, resist a tendency to overintellectualize prayer, as it's more about relationship than results. Seek that relationship with the Lord through his Word and you will understand the context for prayer and how you can grow in that spiritual discipline.
- Relationship Builders: Focus on connecting with the Lord of your life each day. Seek his heart for your life to establish a conversational relationship. You will want a flexible prayer life, but make sure it happens, because you will find harmony and positivity are a natural result of your time with God.
- Influencers: Understand that prayer is the most important thing you can do to influence others and change the world. Carve out the time for it. Find your daily equipping through communicating with God.

- Executors: Determine to arrange your daily life to include prayer. You execute plans carefully, so you can focus on mental and practical strategies that will consistently take you to the throne room in prayer.

## Big-5

The Big-5 Personality Trait assessment is also used widely in business and education, based on a theory D. W. Fiske developed in 1949, on which other researchers later expanded. It works from a framework that can be boiled down to five areas of thinking and these questions:

- Openness: How open and adventurous are you to new ideas and experiences? For example, do you like to take vacations in the same place every year or do you want to experience new places?
- Conscientiousness: How conscientious are you about planning and organizing your life?
- Extraversion: How outgoing and socially oriented are you?
- Agreeableness: How comforting and helpful are you?
- Neuroticism: How visibly moody and anxious are you?[8]

A Big-5 test taker gets a score from 1 to 10 on each of the five areas above. So it's not, for example, a choice between two polar opposites (extraversion vs. introversion), but matters of degree in each of those areas. If you score a 5 on extraversion, that means 50 percent of those who took the test scored lower and 50 percent scored higher. So you're half extroverted and half introverted.

What I find interesting about this schema is the five indicators of personality are focused on outward behavior, as opposed to inner thought life (the focus of earlier tests we've examined). That seems more measurable to me. The Big-5 is not so much about underlying motivation as it is about people's actual conduct. This poses interesting questions: Is personality based on inner thought and motivation or on what we actually do? Is who we are based on our values and ideas about life and self or is who we are based on that which we truly carry out? Am I a prayerwalker if I think about it all the time . . . or am I a prayerwalker only if I actually walk and pray? The answer seems obvious.

But here's another thought on the internal versus external debate regarding personality. People view me as extroverted, but it's not really comfortable for me to jump into large social gatherings. When I taught high school English, I psyched myself up for each class—viewing each class's beginning as getting up on a stage. By three o'clock I was pretty much done with my role as an educational air traffic controller, and I just wanted to shut my classroom door and be alone. (Studies show that teachers are only second to air traffic controllers in terms of the number of decisions they make during a workday.) I joke that I'm a high-functioning introvert. I used to coach my introverted students prior to classroom and senior project presentations by saying, "Yes, I know you're introverted, but for twenty minutes can you pretend you're not? That's what I do every day." So if I *appear* extroverted, am I? If I enjoy entertaining large groups in the comfort zone of my home, am I extroverted? Or am I a closet introvert?

As the Big-5 assessment helps you consider your personality be-haviors, you may find they sometimes create tension with your inner self. This is a big consideration when we think about opportunities for prayer. Our churches would have us pray in groups; that's not a com-fort zone for introverts. Because I'm an inspirational speaker and have written books on prayer, people assume that I love to pray in public settings. But that's not a comfort zone for me either. I'll always pray if asked, but it takes a deep breath and quick prayer before I open my mouth. We should always be mindful that what seems simple to us may take considerable effort for someone else. Fortunately, just like differing personalities, there are a variety of prayer practices that we can celebrate and encourage as beautiful ways to communicate with God.

### ——— PRAYER POINTERS ———

- Openness: If you're adventurous, try various ways to approach prayer—from the labyrinth to prayerwalking to fasting—to change things up from season to season. If you prefer routines, plan a scheduled quiet time and place.
- Conscientiousness: If you're a planner, create that methodology and live it out. If you prefer being more spontaneous, make prayer your objective for the day and intercede as you go.
- Extraversion: If you're outgoing, include others in your prayer life, such as your spouse and kids. If you're introverted, create your safe, quiet spot away from the world to pray.
- Agreeableness: If you tend to be more comforting and helpful, make each day a mission of prayer and intercede for those around you. If your natural instincts are more critical in nature, pray for the problems you notice.
- Neuroticism: If anxiety creeps into your life a lot, turn to God's Word as inspiration for your prayers. Listen to his promises. If you naturally have a more pleasant and peaceful outlook, spend time in praise and thanksgiving.

It's a tricky business figuring out who you are. And even when we're trying to discover our natural praying style, I don't think we can excuse ourselves from praying in a certain manner simply because it's not comfortable for us. Jesus didn't live in a comfort zone. And while he felt it necessary to head up the mountain to have time with God, he also prayed in public. Perhaps it's best if we simply seek God's direction in this matter. He created us. He knows us. And he knows what will be natural for us as we seek a praying-without-ceasing lifestyle.

## ———— DISCUSSION QUESTIONS ————

1. Had you heard of the animal personalities before? Is there one that seems like you?
2. Are you an extrovert or an introvert? How do you know?
3. How do you typically make decisions: with rational data or good instincts?
4. Are you a big picture person or do you tend to focus on the reality, details, and specifics? Think of an example that would explain your answer.
5. Which of the roles and role variants in the Keirsey Temperament Sorter resonate with you and why?
6. What ideas did you find interesting from either the 16 Personalities, StrengthsFinder, or Big-5 summaries?
7. Do any of the Prayer Pointers appeal to you? Which ones and why?

# Chapter 10

# The Enneagram

A PAUSE IS MERITED HERE. I want to state again that I am not advocating for any of the personality assessments in this book. I'm a reporter by nature; I have a journalism degree and try to get to the who, what, when, and where of situations by reading and asking questions. Truly, the best way to know ourselves and God's purposes for our lives is to study his Word. Jesus said to the Jews who believed in him, "If you hold to my teaching, you are really my disciples. Then you will know the truth, and the truth will set you free" (John 8:31–32). We're set free to pursue Christ and his Father's best for our life when we know biblical truth.

At best, personality assessments are theory based on personal observation and study. As with earlier chapters, this one on the Enneagram simply reports what the theory says. I do not endorse it, but I recognize that others have found insight from it that's helped them better themselves and understand others. While any personality test can provide some new perspective, it's imperative to allow the Holy Spirit to reveal truth.

Just as professional counseling can guide us toward healing and growth, personality studies can as well. But we must always allow biblical truth to provide the framework by which we live—not our own experience or any of the various personality assessments. Our goal as followers of Jesus Christ is not to justify our experience, beliefs, and behavior by cherry-picking biblical passages, but instead to allow the truth of the whole Bible to shed light on our lives and transform us from the inside out. One question I'd leave you with is this: Do you spend more time studying and thinking about the Enneagram (or another personality assessment) or the Bible? The latter is the soundest way to understand who you are.

There is a lot of criticism about the Enneagram in Christian circles, so it's important to examine the roots of this philosophy. Those roots come from teachings of Pyotr Ouspenskii (1878–1947), a Russian who expounded on the teachings of George Gurdjieff (c. 1867–1940), who taught that there are three traditional schools or ways—body, emotions, and mind—but that a "Fourth Way" takes one to a higher level of consciousness. Both men were influenced by Eastern thought— Muslim, Buddhist, Hindu—as well as the occult and astrology. Gurdjieff said the Enneagram symbol—which incorporates a circle, triangle, and hexagon—"is a universal symbol" and "all knowledge can be included in the enneagram and with the help of the enneagram it can be interpreted."[1] While many of the Christian faith draw importance in numbers—such as three, seven, or twelve—other forms of numerology that claim to explain human existence are not biblical. These men, however, did not connect their Enneagram thought to human personality.

It was another occultist, Óscar Ichazo, also a student of Eastern religions, who said he developed the nine-point Enneagram through an ecstatic revelation—even before reading Gurdjieff's works. Yet another occultist, Claudio Naranjo, connected these Enneagram teachings to personality types and spread the Enneagram to Catholic contemplative circles, with a former Jesuit, Don Riso, cofounding the Enneagram Institute. From there it spread to a broader audience.[2]

Because I understand the wide popularity of the Enneagram, I decided to include this chapter. Some argue that Christ followers can take the best of a practice and make it their own; others argue that if its original foundation isn't strong, its arguments also will not hold up. Psychology is a man-made science that will always need to be held up against biblical truth for it to have value and influence for our lives.

The basis of the Enneagram is a single question that seemingly arises from Gurdjieff's teachings: Do you think, feel, or act first? Feelers are governed by their heart; they are relationally connected, aware of others' perceptions, and react with emotions. Thinkers are governed by their head; they react with thought, struggle with anxiety, make mental connections quickly, and are good at problem-solving. Instinctive types are governed by their gut; they struggle with anger and justice issues and try to control their environment.

While the classic Enneagram identifies nine types simply by number and without labels, others who teach the Enneagram have attached names to each number. It's also important to note that there is no official Enneagram test. None of its originators created a test that would score people into various Enneagram numbers. Various organizations over the decades have created the Enneagram quizzes that exist today.

The following is a series of fictionalized scenarios that provide a simple summary of each of the personalities.

## Type 1: The Improver

Amara was a school administrator for several years. From a background in business and accounting, she was perfectionistic in nature—with paperwork always caught up. She exhibited strong personal ideals and disciplines, approaching decisions rationally, based on her strong moral character and goal-oriented framework. She wanted to see positive changes in the office professionally and relationally and had the ability to assess how to make those changes happen. She worked hard—often to exhaustion after a fifteen-hour day getting all the details lined up for the days ahead.

A committed Christian, she played the piano (by music, not by ear) at church, read the Bible daily according to a reading plan, and kept careful lists of prayer requests in spreadsheets. Her desire to get everything exactly right kept her in always-striving mode, which may have caused her to miss the message that her worth in God's eyes was not based on performance. If Improvers could relax in prayer and take on a Mary posture instead of a Martha one, they would realize that just as they have a heart for people, God has a heart for them.

## PRAYER POINTERS

- Use a system to list and track prayer requests and answers: notebook, 3" x 5" prayer cards, journal, spreadsheets.
- Put daily prayer time in your planner.

## Type 2: The Helper

I didn't think I needed a second mom, but Aileen did. She pretty much adopted my husband and me, along with our two toddlers, when we moved to the Sierra Valley. When we built our new house from the ground up in our little town, she had to know who we were. So she brought by a pineapple upside-down cake and her big, warm embrace, as well as an open invitation to any of her family gatherings.

When we joined her church, we learned we were nothing special; she pretty much adopted everyone in town and attended all the funerals with at least one covered dish. She had a hard time saying no to her "old people," who often called on her to transport them to doctors' appointments an hour away. But as they were *her* old people, she gave of herself and her resources whenever she saw a need. She lived her life serving others because she loved Jesus and lived out "whatever you did for one of the least of these brothers and sisters of mine, you did for me" (Matt. 25:40). Aileen had long lists of folks who needed prayer and spent countless hours on her knees (until her knees gave out) with eyes closed praying for them.

──────── PRAYER POINTERS ────────

- Recognize that while you love giving to others, the greatest gift you can give them is prayer. Let your doing arise out of your regular quiet time.
- Remember that it's okay and even important to pray for yourself.

## Type 3: The Achiever

When Maxine's students left her class at the end of a period, they often heard her say, "Go, fight, win!"—an expression that certainly portrayed her success-oriented mindset. She was driven to be the best teacher possible, adapting well to changes in assignment because of her determination to succeed and to see her students succeed as well. She was practical, quickly made decisions and plans to implement them, and took pride in her own and her students' achievements. She dressed for success and enjoyed her students' compliments on her clothing. And she was very involved in her church—probably taking on too many responsibilities (simply because she felt she could do them best) and then getting overwhelmed. Maxine's quiet times were like quests—reading and annotating a chapter and then praying for everyone on the prayer list—and she felt great about checking those devo duties off her list each day.

──────── PRAYER POINTERS ────────

- Pray before you jump into your day of planned overachievement.
- In a prayerful listening mode, seek God's input before making commitments and plans.

## Type 4: The Individualist

Everything is a crisis to Lauren. The world is always against her, and while most would see her as self-absorbed, temperamental, and dramatic, perhaps she's simply very sensitive and emotionally based. While critical toward others, if someone criticizes her, she withdraws from the world and sometimes even cuts off relationships. My artistic friend puts her heart and soul into her creations, and praise for her work is probably the one thing that lifts her up and encourages her.

Like the prophet Jeremiah, she prays in laments a lot—not just for herself but also for others around her as her sensitivity puts her in tune with what's going on emotionally within her spheres of influence. Praying those laments by artistically scripting verses in a journal or creating sketches that express her emotions can help her feel she's handed over those concerns to the Lord—and thus fulfilling her emotional need to connect with God.

## PRAYER POINTERS

- Find poetic expression through some form of prayer art.
- Pour your laments out before God. He sees you. He hears you. He will comfort you.

## Type 5: The Investigator

George is probably the most intelligent person I know. He's able to innovatively analyze situations, research solutions, and work out problems to a fiscally sound conclusion. He took a condemned old building and orchestrated its renovation to meet numerous needs in his community. George works best independently, can become lost in his thoughts, and retires to his cave when at home—appearing to be detached from the world's comings and goings—but it's how he recharges.

Nonetheless, when he is working with others, George can appear high-strung and intense. Social situations typically make him uncomfortable, particularly if he knows no one. He is alert and curious, so if he's traveling somewhere, for example, he'll want to know the geographical lay of the land and the history behind the area—and he will read incessantly about the place. George often feels misunderstood and even unappreciated but does not dwell on that probability.

Because he relies on factual information, he read the entire Bible before putting his life in God's hands. It made sense, so he believed and could trust God. His prayer life is simple: when he or a loved one has a need, he prays simply and privately. He doesn't get emotional and so shies away from prayer experiences that seem emotionally based. Even when asked to pray grace over a meal, he is uncomfortable because of the public setting.

### ─── PRAYER POINTERS ───

- Grow in prayer by allowing God's Word to inspire your prayers.
- Be assured that you don't have to participate in group prayer if that is uncomfortable for you.

## Type 6: The Loyalist

Our friend Brian is such a hardworking guy that upon retirement, he immediately jumped into another job just to stay busy. He never misses a day at work and is completely trustworthy, faithful, and loyal to friends and commitments. If we need help with something, he immediately jumps in the car and arrives at our home in minutes. He can quickly diagnose a problem and goes about tasks and cooperative situations with logic and a level head. Brian can get overcommitted because he hates to tell people no, and he might grumble about the stress in his life, but he will also honor and care for others by helping them out. While he is completely competent and gifted, in his prayer life he might appeal to God for help because he sometimes feels insecure or inadequate to a task; prayer and worship alleviate his anxiety.

### ─── PRAYER POINTERS ───

- Try using a prayer app to jump-start your prayer time or consider using a prayer journal such as *Inspired by Prayer: A Creative Prayer Journal*.[3]
- Garner a few trusted friends you can text when you have prayer needs.

## Type 7: The Enthusiast

Helena bounces from one fun activity to the next as she lives life to the fullest. Delight enters the room when she steps in. She's outgoing, playful, and optimistic—with a smile continuously on her face. Because Helena wants to experience everything, she will often take on too much and then feel overwhelmed, and because she's easily distracted and interrupted, tasks frequently remain undone. As a teacher she makes everything fun in her classroom, truly enjoys her students, and breathes optimism into each person she meets. She will drop everything for you because people are important to her. Consequently, it doesn't bother her if the laundry isn't put away or the groceries are still in bags on the counter. Life is an adventure to Helena, so she'll try just about anything. Prayer routines may go by the wayside, and while her prayers are sincere, they often happen on the fly as she's headed from one activity to another.

### PRAYER POINTERS

- Gather your people to pray each day—your immediate family or friends.
- Find fun ways to incorporate prayer with those you love—such as prayerwalks for your neighborhood.

## Type 8: The Challenger

Neil is confident, decisive, and strong-minded. As a manager in a large company, he's in control of all operations and personnel. He is completely sure his decisions are correct, a trait that others find intimidating. He is fearless and takes on huge responsibility, completing management tasks quickly and excellently. However, when situations are not under his control, he can easily get frustrated and angry. Because he's so competent and knowledgeable, people ask for his advice—which is typically sound—and he appreciates being in that kind of mentorship role.

Loyalty is extremely important to Neil, and he is absolutely faithful.

He will protect and defend his family—which they find comforting—and betrayal is his biggest fear. When someone he cares about experiences betrayal, he goes into protective mode, because he has an innate, strong sense of justice and protects those he loves. He enjoys being generous and even heroic in others' eyes.

Neil came to the faith young, then began questioning the foundations of Christianity, but eventually renewed his faith in college. He might resist the vulnerability of prayer because he likes to have all the answers and solutions. But he will humble himself and seek God quietly away from the crowd, submitting to God's protective safe place.

## PRAYER POINTERS

- Take problems to prayer immediately before you get frustrated or angry and before you make decisions.
- Persist in prayer for those prayer needs for yourself and others.

## Type 9: The Peacemaker

Everything is good with Will when there is peace in his surroundings. He is easygoing, agreeable, calm, and open to others and new ideas. While he will typically go with the flow, he can be stubborn about certain ideas if he feels others are trying to control him. To maintain the peace, Will can give in to others' desires so the relationship or work equilibrium is maintained. He's stable, accepting, and trusting, so it's really hard when those he trusts disappoint or even hurt him. Will tends to blend in with whomever he's with—not so much for their approval but instead to keep conflict at bay. He desires to bring harmony, and sometimes he can be complacent and even passive aggressive when there are difficult problems to face and resolve.

An appealing quality of Will's is that he will hear all sides of a story with openness before he makes a judgment. He might often say, "I see where you're coming from," demonstrating respect for the various kinds of people he meets; this gives him the ability to find common ground among an otherwise disparate group. He goes along to get along, allowing other people to make decisions for him until he gets to a tense breaking point, which causes him to step back so as to bring about peace in his own life.

When Will has a tough decision to make, he'll often seek out many counselors who can have great influence on him. He's endearing in faith situations because he is a great supporter of other people and does not need to be in the limelight—he'll take on significant ministry jobs that are hard work but spotlight others. He has vital leadership qualities but waits for others to push him into those positions. His prayer life demonstrates insight into faith fissures, and he prays for God to make life whole and good for others.

### PRAYER POINTERS

- When you go into your natural peacemaking mode, pray. God can bring about unity, peace, and calm much better than anything we can do.
- Know that your prayers are valuable and that God desires an intimate relationship with you that will fulfill your desires for safety and connection.

As you have read these Enneagram scenarios, it's possible you see a bit of yourself in many, if not all, of them. As is true with other personality schemata, Enneagram teachings will tell you that in addition to a dominant type, you will also have secondary types (Enneagram trainers call these "wings") that fill out your personality. Also similar to other personality assessments, you may find that as you take the Enneagram tests that are available, you score differently from one attempt to another. But perhaps some of the prayer ideas in the scenarios above have made sense to you, given the traits that most resonate with you.

The bottom-line question the Enneagram helps us understand about our personality is this: In any given situation do you think, feel, or act first? Feelers are empathizers and emotionally driven; they're innately connected with others and their perceptions of them. Thinkers take time to assess a situation; they rely upon mental connections and look for the problem-solving strategy. Instinctive types are governed by their gut; they need to control the environment and when others who have created the situation struggle, they want to step in quickly to make things right.

As people identify their tendencies, they might see a particular praying lifestyle that makes sense to them. Feelers may need to be in social situations to interact with others in prayer. They care and need to share and pray over others. Thinkers may need to go to God's Word and pray it, or they may want to retire to a quiet place and meditate, listening for the Lord's direction; a labyrinth in their backyard would be a good place for prayer. Instinctives need to move; they may go on a prayerwalk, praying for those they see.

No matter which personality system clicks with each of us, it's important to remember that we should not *follow* any of them. They are made by imperfect humans, they are not scientifically formed, and they are built on people's experiences and observations. As people of faith, we follow God's leading—for our prayer life and spiritual disciplines as well as the other aspects that make up our days.

## ———— DISCUSSION QUESTIONS ————

1. What are your impressions of the Enneagram?
2. Do you tend to think, feel, or act first?
3. Which of the types do you think represents your personality the best? Why?
4. Which one or two others also sound somewhat like you and why?
5. Did any of the scenarios sound like people you know? Explain your answer.

6. Which of any of the personality assessments from the last three chapters seems to make the most sense to you and why?
7. Do any of the Prayer Pointers appeal to you? Which ones and why?

# Chapter 11

# Generational Personalities

ARE YOU A BOOMER OR Gen Xer or Millennial? Or even Gen Z? What do you think that says about you? And are there certain tendencies each generation has in regard to how they pray?

Some have identified the generations as having distinct character-istics and values that potentially influence how they approach prayer; since they grew up with different kinds of church practices, they may have unique comfort zones and understandings about what prayer is. (Note: The dates can differ from one study to another.)

> The Traditionalists—born 1945 and earlier, sometimes re-ferred to as the following:
> The Greatest Generation—born 1901–1927
> The Silent Generation—born 1928–1945
> Baby Boomers—born 1946–1964, sometimes broken into two groups:
> Boomers 1—born 1946–1954
> Boomers 2—born 1955–1964
> Generation X—born 1965–1980
> Millennials—born 1981–1995

Generation Z—born 1996–2015
Generation Alpha—born 2016 and later

Each generation has experienced pivotal world events that may have affected their youth and young adulthood, thus influencing their perspectives and values relating to life, politics, and faith. And they also grew up with different kinds of worship experiences and faith practices common in their time. This chapter will look at each generation and consider how their history could influence their praying life.

## The Traditionalists

The Traditionalist group is often broken down into two distinct generations: The Greatest Generation and The Silent Generation. The former was old enough to have lived during and served in World War II, whereas the latter may have served in Korea or even Vietnam. In fact, The Greatest Generation is also called the G.I. Generation because a large proportion of its young men were drafted into the military during World War II—many women also joined, sustaining production on the home front by entering the workforce in large numbers for the first time. These people also survived the Great Depression of their childhood, and postwar they overfilled colleges with education funded by the G.I. Bill.

My mom and dad met at Syracuse University, which doubled in attendance during 1946—*nine hundred* Quonset huts, barracks, and trailers were added to expand housing and other facilities. Because college attendance rose rapidly, a much-greater-educated population then entered the workforce. My mother said The Silent Generation got its name because those children born during the Depression or World War II were expected to be "seen and not heard."

Technology first exploded during this generation's early adulthood—the telephone, radio, television, and various advanced weapons, including the atomic bomb. Church membership increased during their generation, and parents took their Baby Boomer children to church weekly. It was not a matter of *if* one went to church—but instead a matter of *where* one went to church, with membership at 76 percent of the US population in 1947.[1] The Rev. Billy Graham preached his first crusade in Los Angeles in 1949 to groups across denominational lines and pioneered the use of television to spread the gospel message.[2] In studies during 2016–2018, The Traditionalists were still holding in church membership at 74 percent.[3]

This two-part generation was not generally flummoxed with the spread of COVID-19 because of their ability to accept crisis, adapt to it, and even thrive during struggles. They have demonstrated practicality, a desire for security and even an idyllic life, a hard work ethic, traditional values, and personal discipline. Tom Brokaw's book *The Greatest Generation* fostered the sentiment for the generation's name because of the people's heroism and self-sacrifice during the Depression and World War II. As this generation has been fading in numbers, it is being heralded as leaving the world better than the way it found it.

Traditionalists attended traditional, steepled churches, and families experienced worship services with prescribed liturgies that included hymns. While some prayers may have been extemporaneous, they would likely sound formal in tone to today's listening ears. Personal prayers then emulated what was heard in church. Traditionalists may still use denominational prayer books and say certain prayers that they have memorized for blessings or bedtime or confessional purposes.

Many years ago I organized a prayer ministry at my midsized evangelical church that brought trained intercessors to our church prayer room during Sunday morning to pray for those who desired prayer on their behalf. Those prayer partners from the older generation specifically asked me for a book of prayers they could use as they prayed for others, so I created one to give them confidence in their assignment.

Can a natural praying lifestyle grow out of a practice of using printed prayers? Sure. Just as some people stumble over expressing themselves in conversation, they may also stumble over their prayers—after all, we go to the Living God when we pray! We buy greetings cards that allow us to express our sentiments to those we love. We read the card, we mean the words printed there, and we send it off with a stamp, hoping the recipient believes we truly care. The significant issue in using a printed prayer is a heart one—allowing the in-print lines to become ones we express to our heavenly Father with intentionality and sincerity. What has become the great-grandparent generation (or even great-great-grandparent generation) has prayed with faithfulness and hope for the younger generations. The disciples did not know how to pray, so they asked Jesus to teach them how (Luke 11:1–4); Jesus gave them what we call the Lord's Prayer, a model of how to form our own prayers but also a most excellent one to repeat (complete form in Matt. 6:9–13). If your comfort zone is praying the prayers others have written, that is certainly a good jumping-off place.

### PRAYER POINTERS

- Incorporate prayer books in your quiet time.
- Allow prayers in devotional books to jump-start your own prayers.
- Keep 3" x 5" prayer cards or a prayer list for each of your family members and other loved ones.

## Baby Boomers

The two Boomer generation segments got their name because of the huge population boom after GIs came home from World War II, got married, and settled down. Boomers 1 were born shortly after the war (1946–1954); Boomers 2 were born ten or more years later than their older siblings (1955–1964). The events that influenced their childhood were the Cold War (my family had a large bomb shelter in our Albuquerque home when we lived there one year); the Space Race (moon landing in 1969); the assassinations of President John F. Kennedy

(1963), Rev. Martin Luther King Jr. (1968), and US Attorney General Bobby Kennedy (1968); the Vietnam War (1955–1975) and the peace movement; and the Civil Rights Movement.

Boomers largely grew up in church with their Traditionalist parents and attended college in numbers even greater than their parents had. They highly value communication, and while they have the second highest marriage rate, they also have the highest divorce rate in American history.[4] Boomers inherited their parents' work ethic and are called the workaholic generation, but they're team-oriented and philanthropic in nature.

Jonathan Pontell coined the expression "Generation Jones" for those who were born between 1954–1965. These Boomers did not fully experience the Vietnam-protest era but found that economic concerns such as the oil crisis and stagflation defined their youth and young adult years. Reaganomics influenced them, and they developed a keeping-up-with-the-Joneses, more pessimistic philosophy as some have struggled to keep up with their older siblings.[5]

The most significant faith influence on this generation was the Jesus People Movement of the late 1960s (documented in part with the 2023 film *Jesus Revolution*), which ran into and through the 1970s and phased out in the 1980s. Some have called this phenomenon the Fourth Great Awakening in the US. Hippies, street people, and college students—many of whom had grown disenchanted with the traditional church—found personal faith in Jesus Christ through street preachers and college ministries. They saw people living out faith beyond church walls and learned to read the Bible and pray in ways they had never experienced.

My husband, Craig, and I came into personal relationships with Christ when we were university students. In his first week as a college freshman at UC Berkeley, he met a young man who was on staff with Campus Crusade for Christ (now called Cru), who challenged Craig to read the Bible. My logical, facts-based, decision-making husband read it from cover to cover, decided the Bible was true, and committed his life to Christ.

A year later I went to a free movie with my college roommate at UC Davis (the next year I transferred to Berkeley)—a film called *For Pete's Sake* produced by the Billy Graham Evangelical Association. The title character kept hearing he could have a personal relationship with Jesus. The word *personal* kept hitting me: I had never heard that before. I asked Christ into my life that evening and began studying my white leather King James Bible, which I had never opened other than to look at the pretty, colored pictures. So, the two of us became born-again Christians after having grown up in traditional, mainline churches of formal liturgy. Our lives instantly looked different.

An interesting parallel to this Jesus Movement was the quickly growing Christian publishing industry, feeding the Boomers (and subsequent generations) with magazines and books that helped foster faith. Offerings were mostly nonfiction of a theological bent, with a sprinkling of fiction from C. S. Lewis and J. R. R. Tolkein; Janette Oke's prairie novels weren't first published until 1979. (The Christian Booksellers Association's number of associated stores grew from 211 in 1950 to 1,700 by 2011.[6]) Even the city of Berkeley had a Christian bookstore within a couple blocks of the university campus. Christian organizations with campus outreach, such as Campus Crusade for Christ, InterVarsity Christian Fellowship, and Navigators, all had publishing arms that created Bible studies and other materials that focused on discipleship of new believers. Boomers learned about the Bible and prayer in small-group communities and then plugged in to local churches through their young adulthood.

Prayer shifted for believing Boomers. While they began filling churches, they also went to others' apartments and homes for fellowship and prayer. Worship became more emotionally charged as it changed from ages-old hymns to modern music much like the folk music of the hippie/peace movement—sung to guitars. Prayer was personal, and while the Lord's Prayer may have been said, most prayer times were passionately focused on lifting up needs but also interceding for those who had not come to faith.

As Boomers aged, this generation began writing down prayer requests in black-and-white composition books, notebooks, and journals and even writing out prayers and Scripture promises on a daily basis. Their generation's desire for communication and driven work orientation leaked into their faith, creating spiritual disciplines . . . or guilt when they later struggled to continue them when their married lives became busy.

Today's Boomers may take up various praying lifestyles, and many have also learned the advantages of technology to facilitate a prayerful lifestyle through apps such as Pray.com, an audio app that provides an audio scriptural context for a prayer that follows. Because Boomers are settling into retirement years, their calendars are less stressed, providing more time for spiritual disciplines such as study and prayer.

### PRAYER POINTERS

- Use prayer journals, notebooks, or other organizational strategies.
- Incorporate prayer in daily exercise such as prayerwalking to stay physically and emotionally healthy, as well as to connect with and influence your community spiritually.

## Generation X

A mom saw a book called *Generation X* (written by Jane Deverson and Charles Hamblett) in the mid-1960s, and then her rock and roll son popularized the term by the early 1990s. (It was logical, then, that the subsequent two generations would be Generation Y—more commonly called Millennials—and Generation Z.) Gen X, born from 1965 to 1980, is sometimes called the "forgotten generation" because both their parents were working. Boomer marriages ended in high numbers, and many children became latchkey kids—letting themselves into their homes after school even as young children to wait until their parents returned.

Because of their parents' high divorce rates, Gen Xers started a generational trend of delaying marriage. Like their parents, they have also been workaholics, but they demonstrate a greater sense of life balance—also pursuing leisure with intensity.[7] They're educated and entrepreneurial and grew up as computers first entered workplaces and homes. The founders of Google and Amazon are Gen Xers. Our oldest of four kids did not have a computer in college; her brother, a year younger, did.

In this generation that has seen a slide from denominational church attendance to churches that are not affiliated with any denomination, 56 percent indicate they pray daily, but this figure also includes those from non-Christian religions. Some 25 percent of Gen Xers participate in prayer and/or study groups weekly, 38 percent attend church at least weekly, and 39 percent meditate on a weekly basis. Their desire for work-leisure balance may pan out as recreation on Sundays instead of church attendance.

This group grew up in the hype of the Boomer generation, only to be overshadowed again by hype over studies of the Millennial (Gen Y) generation—hence another moniker, the Missing Generation.[8] Their Jesus Movement parents prayed unrehearsed prayers in public settings, so Gen Xers may have grown up with parents who also prayed spontaneously with them. Gen Xers were encouraged to make public declarations of faith in church settings, youth camps, or youth groups, but many didn't receive faith undergirdings of discipleship. Just as they lost home economics and shop classes in high school and had to figure their way through home management and other life skills, these former latchkey folks have had to make their own paths in spiritual disciplines.

Interestingly enough, hyperactivity diagnoses increased dramatically during the 1990s when Gen X children were climbing into or out of their teenaged years. This increase of ADHD may be due to more accurate assessments, parents' increased awareness, or an increase in the development of ADHD.[9] This could certainly explain a few of those graduating classes I taught! Joking aside, though, some of this task-oriented, hands-on generation may find that prayerful practices that require lots of sitting time might not sync well with their natural disposition toward an active lifestyle. Certainly, their prayers are not missing—even if they seemingly feel their generation has been overlooked.

─────── **PRAYER POINTERS** ───────

- Incorporate prayer in your naturally busy lifestyle of exercise or commuting.
- Set aside some personal quiet time in the early morning or evening when you can share your heart with God.

## Millennials

Much has been made of the Millennial generation. The oldest of this group were coming of age when we turned the calendar to 2000, wondering what might happen. They have been maligned as the Me Generation, partly because of their deep dive into social media that beckoned them to take and post selfies online. But they've never lived without US involvement in a war in the Middle East and have survived two major recessions, the escalation of mass shootings, racial and civil unrest, and 9/11. They were the most racially and ethnically diverse generation until the one that followed.[10]

Economics have given them struggles—high student loan debt (due to rapidly increasing college costs) and high rates of unemployment. They often found upon college graduation that a professional job in their subject area was not available, so they made decisions to delay marriage and children and even home ownership. Lack of job fulfillment has created work-related stress and studies say they may be the first generation that will not outearn their parents.[11] Millennials grew up with computers in the house and had cell phones by the time they were teenagers. Since then they have felt pressure to be connected continually through texting or social media messaging.

While they may be connected with each other through handheld devices, many Millennials conversely feel alienated and lonely. Recent research shows that Millennials are exhibiting higher rates of depression than other generations, due to longer work hours and stagnant wages, with "a severe and persistent low mood, profound sadness, or a sense of despair."[12] Add in societal or self-imposed expectations of creating a vibrant online personality, and Millennials simply may be finding that adult life is not measuring up to the ideals of their youth.

The worship experience for many Millennials has been quite different than that of Gen Xers. Millennials may know church as a former K-Mart warehouse experience with black walls, a stage suitable for a rock star, movable chairs, and light shows. They may also have the expectation that they can disappear into a crowd of thousands—never experiencing *community*, a term they frequently use and desperately desire. Yet in that setting, they may still be plugged in to devices as they're asked to check in, ask for prayer, and take sermon notes.

Fewer Millennials pray, with unaffiliated (nones, unchurched, non-attenders) numbers growing in their generation. Some 39 percent of them pray daily, with 18 percent praying weekly and 7 percent praying monthly. Their prayer time may take place on a handheld device through apps or through music they listen to while walking, cycling, or jogging. They are busy (some working more than one job to make it financially), connected to the world, and yet lonely. Devices, in fact, may be impeding their ability to slow down and have meaningful devotional time.

I sometimes say that I taught the entire Millennial generation. I did teach all the juniors and seniors in our small, rural, public high school who graduated from 1999 through 2014—all the years Millennials would have graduated and headed off to college, the military, or the workplace. The younger two of our four children are Millennials, and I frequently hear from my former students, many of whom ask me privately for prayer. Several dozen of them even contributed to a book I wrote called *50 Life Lessons for Grads*, for which they shared their greatest life lesson experienced during college. A few shared their faith experiences, and I particularly love this generation of young adults for their compassion, honesty, and problem-solving abilities. They are one reason I wanted to write this book. The Millennials as a whole believe in God, in prayer, and in heaven. They're just not sure how to practice prayer . . . or faith, for that matter. For example, because they've grown up connecting online, in-person church attendance may seem irrelevant—although that may be just what they need for the connection they desire.

## —— PRAYER POINTERS ——

- Use prayer apps to kick-start your prayer time.
- Listen to podcasts that pray through the Bible.

## Generation Z

Gen Z, born from 1997 to 2015, is the first digitally native generation. These young adults know nothing of life without cell phones or the ability to access online information with their handheld devices. They are always "on," and they can immediately fact-check statements, making them shrewd and pragmatic. Because of that, their brains have exceptional interconnectivity, and they dominate other generations in terms of their online searches.[13] Their research papers probably have all been done with online sources. Like the Millennials, they've grown up with US involvement in overseas conflicts under the shadow of 9/11, about which they have read or heard but may not remember. Social justice issues have permeated the news of their growing-up years, and many have pursued activism in those issues. Pew Research reports that they are the most diverse generation.

Because church attendance and religious practices have been declining as new generations form, it is no surprise that Gen Z is the least connected to a church experience or spiritual disciplines such as prayer. Their Gen X parents, many of whom chose leisure over formal church services, may have had the view that church attendance wasn't necessary to live out one's faith. And prayer or Bible study may not have formally occurred in the home either. "Seventy-six percent of baby boomers say they had 'meals together as a family' every day when they were growing up, an experience shared by less than half (46 percent) of millennials and only 38 percent of Generation Z."[14] Gen Z largely has two parents working full-time to afford mortgages, car payments, braces, and other expenses of raising children. So family time with meal blessings and prayers may go missing.

Plugged in to their devices continually, Gen Z can be drawn into prayer with meaningful worship experiences that incorporate prayer segments. They most likely are not going to sit around in a circle and pray. Their own issues and passions can be prayer touch points, and mentoring this generation in prayer is critical for faith building blocks and strategies that will help them learn to cope with the challenges ahead.

## PRAYER POINTERS

- Listen to worship music and allow it to inspire your prayer time.
- Investigate prayer apps for younger people.

## DISCUSSION QUESTIONS

1. In what generation were you born? How have others characterized your generation?
2. What do you find appealing about the Traditionalist generations?

3. How did the Jesus Revolution affect the faith of Baby Boomers?
4. How have faith practices changed from the Boomers to Gen X?
5. How would you characterize the faith personality of the Millenial generation?
6. What prayer practices would appeal to those of Gen Z?
7. Do any of the Prayer Pointers appeal to you? Which ones and why?

*Chapter 12*
_____

# Learning Styles

Do we learn differently based on inherent needs and personality? Research is mixed. Many say that learning styles are not valid, and educational communities have pulled away from using assessments that are said to determine learning styles. Much of the issue, it seems, has to do with the validity—or rather, the lack of it—in testing for learning styles. However, most of us have five senses, and I think it can be argued that many of us have preferences as to how we take in and process information.

As a former educator, I know that when I employed sound teaching methodology that incorporated more than one modality, my students learned better. And it may be that we as praying people might prefer one learning or sensory modality over another. Simply put, people might approach prayer differently because of how they process information: visually, auditorily, physically, verbally, logically, socially, and/or solitarily.

## Visual Approaches

Those who prefer visual approaches to learning appreciate visual aids such as pictures, charts, and diagrams. When I'm reading through the books of Samuel, Kings, and Chronicles, I will always search out the charts online that line up the kings and prophets of Judah and Israel. I need that spatial delineation for better understanding. I even created a kings/prophets chart twenty years ago for a Sunday school class I taught that challenged us all to read through the Bible in a year. I also take notes continually during sermons and other speakers' presentations—it helps somehow to see the ideas in my own handwriting that I can scan later.

The challenge with this learning orientation is that I can be very distracted by visual stimuli. I have to shift away from my computer and my phone so that during prayer times I am alone somewhere (my cozy reading chair) to focus on the Lord and listen to his voice. One way I've learned to prayerfully process God's Word is to journal through the Bible. Daily I choose a verse and write it out with colored pencils in the wide margins of Bibles for my grandchildren. Although I'm not an artist, I think of a simple way to convey an idea behind the verse and draw a symbol or picture next to it. As I do this daily, I'm praying for understanding and application for myself, but also for the child who will receive the Bible on his or her next birthday.

I also believe in using prayer reminders. I have a small bulletin board in our hallway with photographs of missionary friends for whom I pray. In the kitchen there are two displays of photos of our family members. Other framed photos around the house, as well as sticky notes, provide reminders to pray for those folks I love. Even art objects inspire my prayers—a vintage print of Irish farmers praying over their potato fields reminds me to pray for my rancher husband who raises hay for his cattle.

Visual distractions need not draw us away from prayer; instead, they can lead us to deeper prayer sensitivity. I learned this when I started prayerwalking for my community. When mental lists started taking over my focus as I walked and prayed, I realized that if I prayed for them, I could then return more quickly to my intercessory mission to pray for the people, businesses, and concerns in my town.

─────────── PRAYER POINTERS ───────────

- Place visual reminders around your home that remind you to pray.
- Create a visualization of your prayer through creative journaling in your Bible or journal.

## Auditory Approaches

I had a few students over the years who didn't take a single note when I was direct teaching. At first it was a bit jarring because I automatically thought they might not be equipped later to take a test on the material. But then they would surprise me by reiterating exactly what I had said. That is a quality of auditory learners.

You might be one if you like to use headphones for virtual classes or meetings so you can focus. Or if you listen to podcasts rather than watch YouTube videos. Or if you prefer audiobooks over print or Kindle versions. When you do have a print book, sometimes you might find yourself reading aloud. And when you're in the car alone, you might have a conversation with yourself. Sometimes that's the most intelligent discussion you have all day, right? Auditory learners prefer getting information auditorily. They may instantly turn on the radio in the car or the television at home. And they may turn to mnemonics a lot to remember lists and important information.

Auditory learners could turn to music to inspire their prayer lives. They might put on their headphones to listen to praise music and be content with singing along prayerfully. Their prayers might be said aloud, and hearing their own words might inspire them to make mental connections that remind them to pray through lists of family members or friends. A mnemonic tool that takes the shape of an acronym such as PRAY could help them say prayers of petition, repentance, adoration, and the yielding of themselves to the Lord's will for their lives. Good listeners are focused and pay attention to what the Lord says, so when they hear of a need they turn to prayer. May we all do that!

─────────── PRAYER POINTERS ───────────

- Speak your prayers aloud.
- Use music or a prayer app on your phone and pray along with the voice artist.

## Physical (Kinesthetic) Learners

The older of my two brothers was always happy when an appliance broke down in our family home. That meant he would get a toaster or even a refrigerator to take apart in the garage to discover how it worked and to see if he could fix it. In the meantime, of course, Mom and Dad had always bought a replacement, but Peter's mechanical abilities only grew—into getting a college degree in diesel mechanics, working as a mechanic, and eventually becoming a manager for the repair shop of a large trucking company. Peter learned by doing. "Learn by doing" is the motto for California Polytechnic University at San Luis Obispo in California—where our two sons got their degrees. They had to not only master challenging coursework but also carry out a senior project that demonstrated their learning. Now they are also managers for corporations.

All people learn best by putting head knowledge into hands-on practice, but some people absolutely require it. They need to experience learning material—put it into practical application or at least think through how something could be personally relevant and lived out. Kinesthetic learners struggle to sit still, and that inspires a question or two. Are our attention spans shortening? Do most of us increasingly find it difficult to sit still because of cell phone notifications pinging us all day long? Personally, I just had to move my cell phone across the room so I could focus better on writing this chapter.

Kinesthetic pray-ers may want to prayerwalk. They want to put prayer into action. They may be the first in the group to lay hands on someone at church and pray for healing. They may also walk through their home or business place touching and praying for those they care about.

Prayer is an experience they need to jump into physically. That may also mean a desire to have a physical worship area in the home, such as an altar with a kneeler. My brother Matt is a golf professional who is constantly on the move. A five-minute phone conversation is a long one for him, because he is wired to move physically to the next experience. He has such a worship area for prayer in his home.

Kneeling is a conscious act of worship many kinesthetic types may need to slow themselves down and focus. Kneeling in prayer is something the Lord leads me to do on occasion—so I'll focus and lift the concerns on my heart. And perhaps a season of kneeling for prayer would be good for us all.

—————— PRAYER POINTERS ——————

- Go for a prayerwalk and praise God for the enjoyment of his creation around you!
- Kneel as you pray to force your body to slow down.

## Linguistic Processors

"Words, words, words," says Shakespeare's character Hamlet in a scene in the castle library. Hamlet is putting on a show of insanity to throw others off, so they think he is not a threat to his uncle, the new king of Denmark, who has murdered Hamlet's father, the former king.

Some may think it is a bit insane that others use reading or writing or talking to process information. But I realized that words truly do help me learn. During a college literature course, I was not understanding the material well. Embarrassingly enough, it was the Bible as Literature class, except that I had only been reading the Bible for a couple years at that point. I went to the final exam shaking in my rain boots but armed with several blue books. While I began writing the essays, the understanding of thematic ideas and threads began to come to me. Instead of a failing grade, I got an A—much to my surprise. Prayer may have had something to do with that, but that experience taught me that I am also a linguistic learner: words are not only how I communicate; they are how I think through and solve problems.

Linguistic learners might consider writing out prayers or using scripted prayer cards. They could also write down prayer requests, keeping track of them in a journal. God can help us process problems by writing out our prayers, and I've had the experience that as I'm talking to God about a need that I have, I suddenly have clarity about what to do. You may find that as well.

### —— PRAYER POINTERS ——

- Write out prayers you create from Scripture.
- Use published books of prayers and say them aloud or write them out for yourself and for others.

## Logical Processors

Logical processors want all the facts. They like systems, procedures, data, rationales for learning, and connections. Factual information proves out the reasons for learning but also shines attention on discrepancies—things that don't make sense or that don't fit.

One of my kids is a logical processor. He questioned his faith going into college; he thought the Bible was not a sound enough foundation to hold together the tenets of Christianity. Of course, as a mom I prayed for him and tried to answer his questions. Then one day I got a phone call. He was taking a course on the history of Christianity, taught by an adjunct professor who was a local minister, and learned about all the ways the Scriptures had been assembled and validated for their authenticity over the centuries. And he believed. Those pieces of data helped him reaffirm his faith.

A logical processor might find help tracking prayer needs through a phone app such as Pray.com. There are many apps that provide prayers, systems for tracking prayer requests, daily Scripture, resources for prayer-related needs, and meditation and sleep helps. Some may prefer their own prayer charts or notebook systems to track requests and answers.

One issue for logical processors is they might get stuck on answers—or the lack of them. We pray, and God answers. Right? Well, not always as we might think. Prayer is not a ratio of faith, and it's not a data-in/data-out kind of process. So the logical thinker might get frustrated. However, one's life of praying has a way of playing out in such a way that we begin to see God's faithful patterns, as well as reasons for what we earlier perceived as unanswered prayer. Then we finally get to that place where we realize prayer is more about access than it is about answers.

It's not a formula; it's all about a deepening relationship of intimacy with the living God who's created us and the world around us. Even a logical thinker will find that understanding is enough.

## ——— PRAYER POINTERS ———

- Devote one journal to prayer requests. Date the request and then write the date and answer.
- Go to God's Word for inspiration on how to pray. Make prayers from the Scripture you read.

## Social Processors

Some students rolled their eyes when I told them they would be working in groups. Others nearly shouted hallelujah. While I formerly was not a fan of group work, I do now dearly appreciate my writing mastermind group. Twice monthly we meet via Zoom to get help with research, writing, and other related business matters. That handful of women has helped me find resources and create meaningful content, as well as blessed me with ideas I had not considered.

Social processors understand that there is power in working collaboratively because you can benefit from the brains and experience of the others in your group. Writers find this to be true through the practice of storyboarding—a dynamic exercise in which an entire book can be conceived and outlined in detail in a couple hours. I've led these exercises many times, and it's rewarding to see others work together as a team. Even introverted types learn to value collaboration.

A natural prayer environment for the social processor (just as with the sanguine temperament) would be group prayer or prayer with another individual. Social processors are filled by and can pour into others with personal interaction. If you have a lot going on, you could include your children and your friends in your prayer time. My daughter recently mentioned her struggle to find prayer time. My suggestion was that she pray with her six kiddos on their hour-long treks twice or more a week to go to music lessons and orthodontist appointments. While the socially oriented person might struggle a bit to put that kind of discipline into place, it is a natural way for not only getting more praying time into a busy calendar but also bringing a family together as a unified unit.

I mentioned before that I lead the prayer ministries at my church. Each Sunday we meet before the first worship service and pray over the church and its leadership. Those who've been involved with prayer ministries are the ones I personally trust the most with my own prayer needs. They are the ones I text or call in a crisis. And even when we cannot be together physically to pray, I sense their presence with me in a heavenly directed prayer room.

You will never feel alone on this earth when you have a group of committed prayer warriors at your fingers' reach.

## PRAYER POINTERS

- Try popcorn prayer with your family at the dinner table, with each person picking the next one to pray until everyone has prayed.
- Gather a group on Zoom weekly for prayer.

## Solitary Processors

On the other end of the social spectrum is the solitary processor. This person prefers to work independently. She prefers study in the quiet of her own comfortable space away from the world. Others in the room may simply be distractions from productive thoughts. I've had students who asked to leave the classroom to work in the library, because even just the noise of pages turning or fingers tapping on a keyboard would keep them from focused work. And sometimes I myself had to leave faculty meetings or trainings when others in the room couldn't stop talking while we were supposed to be writing.

Solitary processors may be emotionally based but they're also visionary in perspective because they have the ability to believe for and visualize answers to prayer. They pray intently in the quiet places of their hearts with dedication to the mission of interceding for family and friends. They may be creatives who artistically render prayer-filled ideas. Noise-reducing headphones could help them get away from the ruckus at home to attend to God's call to pray, and a prayer closet might be a welcomed sanctuary for personal daily retreat and intercession. While solitary processors may appear to live a solitary, inward life, they know they are in the presence of the Lord.

## PRAYER POINTERS

- Create your quiet spot for prayer—with your Bible, journal, and pens ready to go.

- If you have a busy household, face away from others and consider using headphones so you can concentrate.

Understanding our preferred learning styles can lead to a greater understanding of how we might more naturally incorporate increased quiet time with the Lord into our busy, seemingly frenetic lifestyles. And this reminds me . . . now that the house is quiet, I'm heading to my prayer chair to listen for God's guidance in my life!

## DISCUSSION QUESTIONS

1. How do you best receive information that is being taught? Visually? Auditorily? Some other method?
2. Have you used visual prayer reminders? If so, how?
3. Does music inspire a prayerful posture in you? If so, what kind of music facilitates that?
4. What kind of physical praying would appeal to you?
5. Do words help or inhibit your prayers? How?
6. Is there another learning style that intrigues you as it might relate to prayer? Which one and why?
7. Do any of the Prayer Pointers appeal to you? Which ones and why?

# PART THREE

---

*Spiritual Gifts*

*Chapter 13*

# Ministry Gifts

WHILE ALL BELIEVERS ARE CALLED to "pray without ceasing" (1 Thess. 5:17 NASB), they will not live out this prayer calling in identical ways; they've been given unique spiritual gifts that naturally bring about differing prayer practices. Questions to consider in determining your spiritual gifts and how they might relate to prayer are the following (synthesized from John Piper material):[1]

- Why do you do what you do? If you enjoy greeting people at church, for example, perhaps you have the gift of hospitality, because you have the inclination to make others feel welcome and valued.
- What motivates you? If you like to see systems improved, perhaps you have the spiritual gift of leadership. If, however, you take great pleasure in carrying out plans and are good at orchestrating events, perhaps you have the gift of administration.
- Do you do what you do because of love? Do you take on ministry roles because you feel guilty or because you love God, want to serve him, and love serving others?

- Do you want to strengthen others? Spiritual gifts are generally used for the building up of the church. Do you serve because you want to see the body of Christ find spiritual muscle and grow?
- Are you more word-oriented or deed-oriented?

Spiritual gifts are generally divided into three types: ministry gifts, manifestation gifts, and motivational gifts—each used for the purpose of strengthening believers (Rom. 1:11–12). It's my intention that the primary teachings we use as foundations for this discussion come from God's Word. So just as we began this book looking at biblical pray-ers in part one, we'll round out our discussion with the Bible's teachings about various spiritual gifts and consider how they might influence our prayer lives. In this chapter we'll dive into ministry gifts and their prayer applications.

## Prophecy

When authentic prophecy is given to others, it is the "communication of the mind of God imparted to a believer by the Holy Spirit. It may be a prediction or indication of the will of God in a given situation."[2] God uses those with the prophetic gift to give a message to his people for those recipients' "particular need or situation."[3] According to Paul, the gift of prophecy is a manifestation—an outward indication or expression—used for the common good (1 Cor. 12:7), given by Christ (Eph. 4:8) for others' "strengthening, encouragement and comfort" (1 Cor. 14:3). Those with the gift edify other believers (v. 4). Others in the body of Christ benefit and are built up in their faith because of the life-giving words spoken into them.

Good comes out of someone's prophetic statements to others (v. 6). Richard Foster writes:

These are the ones who can envision a new future, a future of righteousness and peace and joy in the Holy Spirit. They are being taken over by a holy power to do the right. They are being brought out of bondage to human beings. They cannot be bribed or manipulated or flattered. They love their enemies and pray for those who despise them. In time their very presence and actions will bring down those structures that are sustained by greed and pride and fear. Their simple noncooperation with the oppression, prejudice, and class strife of modern culture will transform the world almost beyond recognition.[4]

Those exercising their prophetic gifts are encouragers. They comfort and help strengthen the bruised and broken, they speak the truth and reality of God's existence, and they nudge others to step obediently into God's plan for their lives.[5]

Ten years ago I shared a room with a writer friend who has written a dozen books on prayer. As we were talking casually about spiritual gifts, she said, "You *know* you have the gift of prophecy." I laughed and said, "No, I just think I know things." Boldness must be part of the personality equation to step into that calling. Once in a while I will have a strong impression that I am supposed to speak life into someone, such as one time in church when I told a visitor, "I sense that God wants me to tell you that he loves you and will see you through whatever you are going through right now." She received that well and seemed lightened. Those with prophetic gifts lighten others.

But I once had an uncomfortable experience receiving a prophetic word. When I visited my daughter's church in Honolulu, the pastor invited others with prophetic giftings to speak from the stage after the service. Earlier my daughter had introduced me to a young female friend sitting directly in front of us. When I saw that she was the first to speak, I knew she would have words for me.

Sure enough, she pointed me out in front of the hundreds attending, said my name, and said I should not worry because God would take care of any concerns I had about my health. Embarrassed in front of people I did not know, I wondered—as I still do—why she hadn't simply turned to me privately and said the same thing.

It's no wonder that Paul wrote about the importance of women covering their head while prophesying; his point was certainly designed to indicate that prophetic speaking should not be a show and we (both women *and men*) should not draw attention to ourselves.

Prophecy and prayer go hand in hand. Those with the gift have not only been reading Scriptures but also know them. They settle into prayer times with a listening heart, eager to hear God's direction and encouragement for their own lives, and for others as well. They pray big, beyond-their-reach prayers as they intercede on behalf of others. They can't just "know things" (my brother calls me "Bossy Big Sister") but must also have compassionate hearts.

Paul wrote that his readers should follow the way of love and eagerly desire gifts of the Spirit, "especially prophecy" (1 Cor. 14:1). Those gifted with prophetic encouragement have an undergirding of God's love for others and speak promise into others that they themselves have prayerfully heard. They don't rush prayer times but wait for God's words (which may not sound like their natural form of speech) and a heightened sense of his presence.

## PRAYER POINTERS

- Set aside quiet time for listening, so you can clearly hear God's voice.
- Write down what you hear from God, and pray about how that might encourage others.

## Teaching

Teaching is a tough calling. To James's statement that not many should become teachers because "we who teach will be judged more strictly" (James 3:1), I shout a hearty "Amen!" While I did not teach overtly

Christian content at our public high school, God did call me to teaching and developed the gift in me so that I could convey challenging content—much of which conveyed spiritual themes and examined literary works written by people of faith. But I had textbooks to help me, while the New Testament writers had only the *Tanakh*, the Hebrew Scriptures. And yet those messengers were critically important to the formation of orthodox Christianity—the correct, biblical concepts that teach who Jesus was and is and what he did.

Paul wrote that we receive the different gifts according to the grace given us. Those with the spiritual gift of teaching have a serious responsibility to impart truth about the Christian faith. It's important to be grounded in the Scriptures in order to be spiritually mature, to have correct understanding about who Christ is, and to teach others effectively and correctly. Without solid teaching, Paul warns us, we are faith infants, "tossed back and forth by the waves, and blown here and there by every wind of teaching and by the cunning and craftiness of people in their deceitful scheming" (Eph. 4:14). And Peter warns that there will be false teachers (2 Pet. 2:1); certainly, we can observe personalities in the Christian world who are successfully drawing audiences with easy, comfortable diets of spirituality that do not necessarily line up with scriptural truth.

Along with preachers, those who teach have double honor (1 Tim. 5:17). Why? First, because it's hard work: it requires reading and studying and deep reflecting. Good teachers do more than relate truth; they connect with others and teach in such a way that the biblical concepts go deeply into one's mind, heart, and soul. I still remember a teacher who explained the various impediments to prayers being heard and answered; I could list those still today, decades later. Teachers also need to show integrity; they cannot just know the Scriptures—they have to live them out (Titus 1:8–9). The writer of Hebrews taught that "by this time you ought to be teachers" (Heb. 5:12), from which we can infer that this gift is something into which we can grow. As with any spiritual gift, though, the Lord's anointing will guide us in our calling (1 John 2:27).

How do those with the gift of teaching pray? Humbly. Continually. Sometimes desperately. As someone who has taught in the public schools but also taught Bible studies, spoken before many audiences, and written a passel of books, I pray from word to word. As I prepare to teach—in any venue—I'm continually at the throne begging for the right words to be conveyed in a manner that is true, understood, meaningful, applicable, and visible in my own life. Daily I pray over the Scriptures I read, asking God for just the right verse to post on social media and to guide that day's blog. Immersion in truth begets prayer—prayer for my own new understanding of how I can grow in prayer for those who will receive the word.

Scripture literally forms the basis of a short, daily prayer I share with my online Bible Girls group that reads through the Bible each year. And the focus verse stays with me throughout the day—challenging my bad attitudes, helping me prioritize my day, and keeping me grounded as a teacher. It's a posture at the cross, and when on my knees at the cross, there's a desperate sense that the moments of the day ahead are not worth much unless I place them into God's hands. If teaching does not inspire prayer, that person should not teach.

## PRAYER POINTERS

- Allow prayer to grow out of the study of God's Word.
- Pray before each and every teaching session.

## Apostleship

People who establish churches are called apostles. We see this term used in Scripture when Jesus prayed through the night and then "called his disciples to him and chose twelve of them, whom he also designated as apostles" (Luke 6:13). Mark described their work thus: "that they might be with him and that he might send them out to preach and to have authority to drive out demons" (Mark 3:14–15). (Later Matthias was added to replace Judas, we read in Acts 1:25–26.) Jesus's apostles were committed to following him physically and otherwise for training, the practice of ministry, and intimate fellowship with him.[6] The Greek word is *apostolos*, which means *apo* or "from" and *stello* or "to send."[7] Apostles are sent ones or messengers. Their message is the gospel of Jesus Christ, who was the very first apostle: "whom we acknowledge as our apostle and high priest" (Heb. 3:1).

John also used this term when he wrote "and Jesus Christ, whom you have sent" in his Priestly Prayer (John 17:3). The Lord God, the Father, sent Jesus, and then Jesus sent the apostles: "Therefore go and make disciples of all nations, baptizing them in the name of the Father and of the Son and of the Holy Spirit, and teaching them to obey everything I have commanded you" (Matt. 28:19–20). The purpose of the apostles was to establish churches (Eph. 4:11–12). They provided a foundation of teaching for early believers, with Jesus himself as "the chief cornerstone" (Eph. 2:20).

Can there be apostles today? Yes. The use of the term *apostle* expanded with Paul, whom Jesus commissioned directly—a commissioning confirmed as Paul established and mentored churches among non-Jewish peoples. Later, many others were called apostles: Barnabas, Andronicus, Junias, two unnamed brothers, Ephaphroditus, Silas, and Timothy. Just as these original apostles bore witness to the gospel message, today's apostles study Scripture and experience the Lord's transforming power in their own lives. They not only tell the story (Gal. 2:7–9), but also provide a foundation for the building up of a church. Today church planters would have the spiritual gift of apostleship. Apostles now, just as they were in the early church, are "pillars" of faith (v. 9).

When we're trying to understand how apostles might naturally pray, we have several great examples, including Jesus, Jesus's half brother James, Peter, Paul, and John. We know that Jesus sought out quiet time with his Father away from the crowds. He also prayed spontaneously in response to situations and prayed for both others and himself; his longest recorded prayer, found in John 17, primarily focuses on intercession for his followers and those who would later believe. In all his letters Paul indicated that he prayed continually, and because he often mentioned the individual needs of the churches to which he was writing, we can be assured he saw prayer as a problem-solving solution—lifting up those needs and trusting the Lord for them.

In his letter James demonstrated a similar mindset to that of Paul. Prayer was an organic outflowing of his daily walk. Got a problem? Go to prayer.

- Do you need direction and wisdom? Ask God in faith. (James 1:5–8)
- Are you quarreling and fighting because you don't have what others have? Ask with the right motives. (James 4:1–3)
- Do you feel distant from God? Draw near to him by resisting the devil. (vv. 7–8)
- Are you overwhelmed with grief? Humble yourself before God. (vv. 9–10)
- Are you in trouble? Pray. Are you happy? Praise God. Are you sick? Ask for prayer. (James 5:13–15)
- Feeling guilty? Confess your sins to each other and pray for each other for healing. (v. 16)

This was one of Jesus's half brothers who did not believe in him until after the resurrection, but became a praying-without-ceasing apostle. Apostles like James would be in constant problem-solving mode relating to the message of the gospel, facilities and their many issues, discipleship, and the development of leaders who would become followers of Jesus Christ and pastors. They would certainly be praying in advance, praying behind the scenes, and praying on the go.

## PRAYER POINTERS

- Pray regularly with trusted leaders about how to advance God's kingdom.
- Have concerted listening-prayer times with an open journal or Bible to record insights or God's direction.

## Evangelism

In a listing of spiritual gifts written to the Ephesians, Paul mentioned apostles and evangelists separately, although certainly many could have both gifts. The missions of the apostle and the evangelist seem to navigate the same road: the spread of the gospel. But there's one small difference: evangelism is perceived more as a function than an office.[8] The position of apostle implies leadership; that of the evangelist does not. Philip (also an original disciple and apostle) served as an evangelist in Caesarea (Acts 21:8); he was one of seven the disciples appointed to meet the prayer and physical needs of the people (Acts 6:1–6). Philip exhibited the gift early. In John 1:43–51 we learn that Jesus was on the east side of the Jordan River when he found Philip and said, "Follow me" (v. 43). Philip immediately found Nathanael and told him he'd found the one written about in the Law and the Prophets. Then when Jesus approached Nathanael and said he had seen him under the fig tree before Philip called him, Nathanael believed and followed Jesus too. Philip—the only New Testament character actually called an evangelist—instinctively knew Jesus was the Messiah and was ready to share that good news.

The word *evangelist* in the Greek comes from *eu* or "well" and *angelos* or "a messenger." Thus, the word means "a messenger of good."[9] And *gospel* means good news, so it makes sense that the evangelist's gift is used to share the good news. Evangelists also help the church grow in numbers and prepare God's people for works of service (Eph. 4:12).[10] The word *evangelist* is only used three times in the New Testament, including this verse in 2 Timothy 4:5:

> But you, keep your head in all situations, endure hardship, do the work of an evangelist, discharge all the duties of your ministry.

In that letter to Timothy, imprisoned Paul encouraged his fellow worker and spiritual son to guard the gospel, keep on sharing the good news, and suffer for its sake, if necessary.

Evangelists pray forward. They are coffee-mug-half-full kinds of people. They see possibilities in people and communities and pray with faith for open doors and open hearts and minds. These people pray bold prayers because they have a bold mission: to share the gospel in such a way that people leave darkness for light.

Change is hard for people; it implies that people have been in error and sin—so it's hard to shift thinking. But evangelists understand the dramatic difference. In the same way Jesus prayed, they would pray believers may be "brought to complete unity." Then others of the world would know God sent his Son Jesus and loves them as God has loved his Son (John 17:23). They see people and pray them to the kingdom because of their passion for Jesus.

─────────── **PRAYER POINTERS** ───────────

- Prayerwalk your community, praying for each person in every household, business, school, or government office to profess their faith in Christ.
- Fast and pray before exercising your gift.

## Shepherding

Another spiritual gift is shepherding, more commonly called *pastoring* in our vernacular. In fact, when Paul identifies some of the gifts in Ephesians 4:11, the Greek word he uses, *poimen*, means "shepherd"—one who tends herds or flocks. *Pastor* has the same Greek origin, and in most common Bible translations, we will find the word *pastor* in that verse, the only time we will see *pastor* used in the New Testament. So there's not a lot of guidance for us about what tasks someone with this gift would take on—unless we go back to teachings in the Gospels when Christ used the metaphor.

But first I'd like to share a few experiences about sheep. My oldest raised sheep, and we quickly learned a couple things about them. They need watching and guiding. One day when I was away, my daughter brought her lamb to our fenced backyard, so she could groom it and work with it. Then she left the lamb for a while when she went inside the house. When I got home, all of the flowers on the expensive perennials I had just planted were gone! Sheep also need boundaries. They will wander from green spot to green spot if fences and gates are not secure—and they're pretty good about wiggling through them.

One day when I was prayerwalking near the schools, I saw the high school sheep herd munching on the football field. Try as I might, I couldn't get them back to their own pasture at the school. So I called Bill, the agriculture teacher, who was there in minutes because he lived just a couple houses away. With one word—"Home!"—the sheep beelined back into their pasture. And that experience illustrates two more points: the shepherd drops everything for the sake of the sheep, and his sheep know his voice. Those sheep would not listen to me, but they immediately knew their shepherd's voice and knew exactly where to go.

Jesus must have known these shepherding principles, as he used them to help others understand his role as the Good Shepherd. "When he saw the crowds, he had compassion on them, because they were harassed and helpless, like sheep without a shepherd" (Matt. 9:36).

We see his pastoral compassion when he fed the five thousand and then the four thousand a short time later. This is what pastors do—give spiritual food to their flock, their people. The writer of Hebrews notes Jesus's shepherding role as well, in a benediction toward the end of his letter:

> Now may the God of peace, who through the blood of the eternal covenant brought back from the dead our Lord Jesus, that great Shepherd of the sheep, equip you with everything good for doing his will, and may he work in us what is pleasing to him, through Jesus Christ, to whom be glory for ever and ever. Amen. (Heb. 13:20–21)

If pastors model their shepherding after Jesus, they will equip their people with what they need to follow God's will. And pastors' families will testify that their spouse or parent certainly lays a lot down for the sake of the church, just as Jesus said the good shepherd lays down his life for his sheep (John 10:11).

Peter's charge to elders at the end of his first letter provides insight into what pastors may still struggle with today:

> Be shepherds of God's flock that is under your care, watching over them—not because you must, but because you are willing, as God wants you to be; not pursuing dishonest gain, but eager to serve; not lording it over those entrusted to you, but being examples to the flock. (1 Pet. 5:2–3)

He continued to encourage his readers to be submissive and humble, cast anxiety on God, be self-controlled and alert, and resist the devil (vv. 5–9). This is an image for servanthood in leadership of churches or parachurch organizations.

Guiding, teaching, overseeing—these are heavy responsibilities to take to prayer, along with the myriad of needs from the people a pastor serves. As a young pastoral candidate, Eugene Peterson thought the bulk of his work would be developing a prayer life among the church people. He was surprised, however, when nothing was mentioned about prayer in the job description and later determined that "being a physician of souls took priority over running a church."[11] A vibrant prayer life is likely a pastor's priority, but it may be hard to attain.

While pastors' intent may be to have long, uninterrupted daily prayer times, a long list of administrative tasks might pull them away from that important centering. Meetings and emergency hospital visits, counseling appointments and Zoom conferences can fill up a calendar. But the food their sheep need requires focused time in prayer for insight, direction, and intercession.

It is reported that Martin Luther once said he had to work from early to late. "In fact, I have so much to do that I shall spend the first three hours in prayer."[12] Pastors will have different personalities: some will be extroverted and social, while others will be more studious and introverted. However, their calling to shepherd people is such an immense weight that prayer certainly will be their greatest armor other than God's Word.

─────────── PRAYER POINTERS ───────────

- Make sure you have a prayer team that prays with you regularly.
- Pray Ephesians 6:10–20 on a daily basis, and memorize this and other equipping passages.

## Helping

Many years ago I felt the tug to help a nonprofit organization called Awaken in Reno, Nevada, which helps women and children get out of the sex trafficking industry. I went through the training, thinking that I could assist with teaching or doing college and financial aid advisement, or even some speaking. After the training session, however,

I found that what the organization really needed was meal preparation and even an occasional decorated cake. The leaders and social workers simply did not have time to prepare meals for the special events and birthday parties. So I began prepping meals, and since I learned to decorate cakes for our slew of kids and grandkids, I provided those too.

I was reminded of this recently when I read about the disciples' dilemma in Acts 6. The church was growing significantly, and the disciples were preaching in public and dealing with the fallout of criticism. One incident was even inside the church. The Grecian Jews complained that the Hebrew Jews were exhibiting favoritism in the distribution of food—favoring the Hebrew widows but overlooking the widows of Grecian origin. The twelve disciples met and determined they didn't have time to supervise this aspect of the ministry, so they chose seven men to take care of those tasks and even ordained them: Stephen, Philip, Procorus, Nicanor, Timon, Parmenas, and Nicolas from Antioch (Acts 6:5; notice all the names are Greek). This delegation of work would allow the disciples to focus on preaching and teaching.

The seven men delegated to this work had the spiritual gift of helping—"supporting or assisting members of the body of Christ so that they may be free to minister to others."[13] The focus of serving would be ministry to the poor, needy, sick, and distressed—as we see with the mention of the widows of those two cultures. Specific tasks could be anything that would meet the very real needs that leadership or administration simply could not manage.

Greek words for *helping* are *antilepsis* (or *antilempsis*), which means "laying hold of or an exchange"—for the underlying purpose of support.[14] Those with the spiritual gift of helping step in to assume an exchange: they take over what someone else cannot do so as to meet the needs of ministry and others. A disciple in Joppa who clearly had the gift of helping was Tabitha (also called Dorcas); we learn she was always doing good works and helping the poor (Acts 9:36).

As the body of Christ continued to grow, certainly the needs multiplied as well—requiring more people with the gift of helping. Paul instructed Timothy to advise families of widows in the Ephesian church to care for their own widows, so that the church could help those widows without family to help (1 Tim. 5:16). To this day, when people don't have families nearby, they often turn to their church for help.

We see in our own churches how these kinds of helping ministries grow. My church has many gifted in helping. We provide food for hundreds of families through our food bank. Another ministry does simple car repairs and maintenance for those who cannot afford such work. Our church also provides our former parsonage building rent-free to a nonprofit called Project 150, which uses the building as a boutique with clothing for homeless teens. Additionally, the church donates generous outdoor space for several nonprofit organizations partnering together to create community gardens that serve the Boys and Girls Club next door, our own food bank, and other needs in the community. While there are leaders for these ministries, there are also many helpers.

Helpers usually cannot sit still. They have instinctive radar for the needs around them and step in to make others' work lighter. They pray on the go. Some may sing praise as they work. Others may work more quietly and see their work as a form of meditation and offering to the Lord. At a recent event I organized, a friend came early and said, "What can I do? Put me to work." After the event was over, she said, "I was praying this morning, and God simply nudged me to come and help you. I know you don't delegate well, so I figured there would be something for me to do." I had to laugh. She was absolutely right.

─────── **PRAYER POINTERS** ───────
- Pray as you go throughout your day.
- Remember to allow some quiet time to pray for yourself and to listen to God's encouragement to you.

———————— DISCUSSION QUESTIONS ————————

1. How would you answer the five bulleted questions in the introduction?
2. How should prayer connect with the gifts of prophecy and teaching?
3. In his letter how did James demonstrate the importance of prayer to solve problems—some of which could certainly relate to apostleship—a gift of those who establish churches?
4. The author writes, "Evangelists pray forward." What do you think that means?
5. How might someone with the gift of pastor rely on prayer?
6. How would you characterize those with the gift of helps and the ways they might pray?
7. Do any of the Prayer Pointers appeal to you? Which ones and why?

*Chapter 14*

# Manifestation Gifts

SOME SPIRITUAL GIFTS ARE CALLED manifestation gifts because they provide an outward manifestation of the supernatural power of the Holy Spirit. They are an outward expression for the benefit of others. Paul lists them in 1 Corinthians 12:8–10: wisdom, knowledge, faith, healing, miracles, discernment, speaking in different kinds of languages (tongues), and interpretation of tongues. (Paul also listed prophecy here, but we've already discussed that gift in the last chapter.) In this chapter, we'll examine the natural praying practices that tend to accompany each of these gifts.

## Wisdom

Wisdom is more than just a desirable human characteristic; it's also a spiritual gift. Paul wrote, "To one there is given through the Spirit a message of wisdom" (1 Cor. 12:8). This is a manifestation gift because there is a message involved. The individual is not simply a wise person; she conveys the wisdom given to her from the Holy Spirit. Paul wrote extensively about this gift in the second letter to the Corinthians, in which he's trying to clear up many of the Corinthian church's misconceptions and wrong practices regarding the faith.

The gift of wisdom is not mere human eloquence or the wisdom of the age or its culture or its rulers. Paul's wisdom focused on the subject of his teaching and preaching: Jesus Christ. He wrote that he was weak, but that the Spirit is powerful and helps us understand what God has freely given us. Just as no one can know my thoughts, no one can know God's thoughts except the Spirit, who searches for all the deep things of God. Those with the gift of wisdom are blessed with God's secret wisdom, which is designed for our glory; so like Paul, they speak spiritual truths that the Holy Spirit gives them. Paul wrote, "We have the mind of Christ" (1 Cor. 2:16) and that in our human understanding we cannot summon wisdom because

What no eye has seen,
    what no ear has heard,
and what no human mind has conceived—
    the things God has prepared for those who love him.
(1 Cor. 2:9)

God's truth will be foolishness to those who do not believe, but it will benefit believers.

Wisdom is a gift worth seeking, and that seeking comes through prayer. To the Ephesians Paul wrote, "I keep asking that the God of our Lord Jesus Christ, the glorious Father, may give you the spirit of wisdom and revelation, so that you may know him better" (Eph. 1:17). In faith we can ask God for wisdom, as James wrote in his letter to the twelve Jewish Christian tribes, because God will give it generously to all without finding fault (James 1:5). And the result of that wisdom will be a life lived rightly and deeds accomplished humbly.

Those with the gift of wisdom pray. They know their wisdom comes through the power of the Holy Spirit. They know they *don't* know, so they ask God, who gives generously. And this is serious business, because their words are God-given for the sake of speaking truth into other believers. They listen in prayer, so this is not a hurried process, and they're willing to sit still in silence—a prayer corner or closet—so the world around them doesn't interrupt this impartation.

—————— **PRAYER POINTERS** ——————

- Use the Bible as a springboard for prayer so any wisdom is truly from him.
- Set aside a weekly time simply for listening prayer. Have a Scripture focus, then wait for God to speak to you.

## Knowledge

Maxine was sitting around a conference table with numerous others interviewing a prospective pastor who'd brought his wife with him for the intense weekend meeting with the pastoral search team and others from the church. As committee members asked questions and the gentleman responded, Maxine knew something was true: her future best friend was sitting across the table from her. With God's leading, the church committee hired the new pastor and that friendship quickly formed; they are still the closest of friends today.

That kind of understanding results from the spiritual gift of knowledge, which meets the need of the Christian community when knowledge or wisdom is required for making decisions or choosing proper courses of action.[1] Paul mentions this gift four times, all in his first letter to the Corinthians, who as we remember were spreading false teaching.

- "To one there is given through the Spirit . . . a message of knowledge by means of the same Spirit." (1 Cor. 12:8)
- "If I have the gift of prophecy and can fathom all mysteries and all knowledge, and if I have a faith that can move mountains, but do not have love, I am nothing." (1 Cor. 13:2)

- "Love never fails. But where there are prophecies, they will cease; where there are tongues, they will be stilled; where there is knowledge, it will pass away. For we know in part and we prophesy in part, but when completeness comes, what is in part disappears. . . . And now these three remain: faith, hope and love. But the greatest of these is love." (vv. 8–10, 13)
- "Now, brothers and sisters, if I come to you and speak in tongues, what good will I be to you, unless I bring you some revelation or knowledge or prophecy or word of instruction?" (1 Cor. 14:6)

We learn several principles from these passages about this manifested gift.

First, just as with wisdom, it is the Spirit who gives knowledge. It's not just something that the human brain comes up with; it's a supernatural gifting made possible only because of one's surrender to the Holy Spirit's interior work. Next, love must be the foundational motivation in sharing this gift with other believers. It's not to be a showy gift. We don't run around puffed up, all proud of ourselves because we know things. Lastly, knowledge has value for the body of Christ because it's a message from God that will provide clarity and direction.

There are many Greek words that are translated as *knowledge* in the New Testament—with many other connotations. The one that Paul used is *gnosis*, which means "a seeking to know"—an inquiry, investigation, knowledge, especially as the context relates to spiritual truth. It also means a "word of knowledge," which is the term many use.[2] They might say, "I have a word of knowledge I would like to share." In all cases, that word would never be contrary to Scripture's teachings. It's a gift that humbles, not elevates.

A praying-without-ceasing lifestyle quietly builds confidence and boldness into the person who has the spiritual gift of knowledge, so there will be a sense of freedom in speaking God's message to the body of Christ. That's a moment-by-moment sense of the presence of

God. Scheduled and executed prayer time is essential, but a running conversation—seeing God's hand in everything—would be more conducive to sensing that word of knowledge.

——————— **PRAYER POINTERS** ———————

- Pray God gives you insight—that special word of knowledge— and then seek his direction about what to do with that word.
- Seek God from the moment you get up—noticing what he is doing in the world.

### Faith

The whole Bible is a collection of faith stories, but there is a different kind of faith too—the spiritual gift of faith, which Paul includes in the list of 1 Corinthians 12: "to another faith by the same Spirit" (v. 9). The Greek word *pistis* conveys a conviction based on hearing, always of faith in God, Christ, or things spiritual.[3] This faith is different than saving faith; instead, those with this gift have a "confidence in the power and promises of God that they can stand strong in their belief, no matter what may try to shake them."[4] This faith defends and advances the cause of Christ.

One of the greatest examples of someone with the gift of faith was George Müller, the well-known orphanage founder and director who lived in 1800s England. He never solicited funds for the expenses involved in raising hundreds of orphans over the years. Instead, he prayed, and provision would drop into his hands. He didn't have just one or two orphanages—he had nine different facilities—and he also sent 10,000 pounds (English money) annually to nearly two hundred missionaries during the 1870s (roughly $300,000 in US dollars today). Müller also preached to three million people starting in the mid-1870s, traveling to forty-two countries over 200,000 miles.[5] He eventually wrote that he knew of at least 50,000 specific answers to his prayers.

At the start Müller prayed that God would provide a house for the first orphanage, for someone who would pay the rent or give such a house to him, for furniture, for clothing for the children, and for "suitable individuals to take care of the children." This prayer was on December 5, 1835. Five days later he got a letter from a brother and sister who proposed they provide the furniture and themselves to do the work for no salary. Three days later, another person committed to provide the rent.[6] Books have been filled with stories of Müller's faith prayers that came to fruition, documented with his own narratives.

The gift of faith believes God will answer and provide, and prayer is a vehicle for moving those visions forward. Romans 10:17 says, "So then faith comes by hearing, and hearing by the word of God" (NKJV). Those with the gift of faith completely trust in the Lord because they know God's Word, they know its promises are true, and they believe in and see God's hand in their lives—and the lives of others. Each day I read a chunk of the Bible from my read-through-in-a-year plan and write a prayer based on the Scripture I have read. Year after year, I read the stories of God's faithfulness to his people, and year after year my faith grows. For those who desire the gift of faith, I suggest reading the Bible from cover to cover and spending time daily in prayer, pondering God's faithful, gracious character.

——————— PRAYER POINTERS ———————

- Read the Bible and write out prayers for people that are based on God's Word.
- Keep a prayer list of BIG prayers and pray daily for them, expectant of God's good answers.

## Healing

In the days I have been writing this book, I have witnessed a healing—that of a beloved relative. Two days after a major surgery for her third incident of abdominal cancer, her heart stopped, and she was non-responsive for ten to twelve minutes. A medical team brought her back to life and she had a second surgery for internal bleeding, which had caused her heart to stop. She is now well at home.

Was this healing of medical science or of God? Russell Moore writes, "God still heals and God still heals in extraordinary ways. I think one thing that Christians sometimes get confused about is they assume that you have regular healing (ordinary healing) and extraordinary healing." Moore says any healing is extraordinary, and the Bible doesn't tell us that God will stop working in extraordinary ways.[7] Most likely you have heard of others being healed. Moore claims that all believers' prayers for healing are answered—some with life still left here on earth and some with life eternal.

Let's look at Paul's statement about this gift: "For to one is given through the Spirit the word of wisdom; and to another the word of knowledge, according to the same Spirit: to another faith, in the same Spirit; and to another gifts of healings, in the one Spirit" (1 Cor. 12:8–9 ASV). This plural expression of the gift, *healings*, is the literal word Paul wrote—one that's usually translated as a singular word, *healing*—perhaps indicating that those with the gift would heal different illnesses, not just one.[8] The Greek word, *iama*, means "to heal" and "made whole," including spiritual healing, and is different than the word used for treatment or therapeutic care of the sick (*therapeuo*). God gives the gift of healing, and God does the healing through that person.

Jesus healed, and Jesus gave authority to drive out evil spirits and heal every disease and sickness (Matt. 10:1). Healing came through others touching him (Luke 6:19), Jesus touching them (Matt. 8:3), a word from Jesus (v. 13), a touch of his garment (Mark 5:28), and even Jesus's spit (Mark 7:33–35). These examples are a few of many. Luke, the disciple who was a physician, used the word *healing* the most—fifteen times. Life is in God's hands, isn't it? So, healing is in God's hands as well.

None of us is a healer, but God has gifted some to become part of his healing process. My relative had five surgeons God used to bring about healing; they found two tumors instead of the one technology found, and they saved her only remaining kidney when it was earlier thought she would lose it. I believe God was in that surgical room those many hours, using their eyes and hands.

How would those with the gift of healing pray? Jesus prayed up the hillside from Capernaum away from the crowds. And he prayed authoritatively on the spot; he removed demons, and people walked away whole. His work was prayer; his prayers were part of his work. Those with healing gifts pray with their eyes and hearts. They see others in need—whether in person or not—and they pray. They scroll through social media, see requests for prayer, stop, and intercede. They touch others—figuratively and literally—and God restores wholeness.

I got a phone call one day. The caller said, "I heard you're praying for my wife."

I immediately thought, *Uh-oh, I'm going to get an earful.* I'd heard his wife was losing her eyesight to macular degeneration, and I had been praying for her. I said, "Yes, every time I walk by your business I pray. How is she doing?"

"Well, I just want to thank you. She is really improving and is back driving again. I knew it must be your prayers."

"No, sir," I said, "I just pray. God does the work."

Prayer puts the problem and the person in God's hands. And whether we feel we have the gift of healing or not, we can trust him, because he is the Great Physician.

─────────── **PRAYER POINTERS** ───────────

- Pray as a response to learning of others' illnesses—online and personally.
- Take Jesus's statement seriously: "This kind can come out only by prayer" (Mark 9:29). Use Jesus's words in prayer for healing.

## Miracles

We throw around the expression "It was a miracle!" frequently in our everyday conversations. Paul also lists "miraculous powers" in 1 Corinthians 12:10 as another of the spiritual gifts. The literal translation is "deeds of power," because the Greek root for miraculous is *dunamis*, which is power or might as seen through works of a supernatural origin and character. These phenomena are not produced by natural means and are intended as evidence of God's power and purpose.[9]

There are two kinds of miracles we see in the Bible: healings and other works that control nature. When we think of Jesus's miracles, all the healings come to mind, but there were many other miracles he performed: water turned into wine at the Cana wedding, two miraculous catches of fish, two feedings of the multitude, walking on water, calming the storm, finding the coin in the fish's mouth, and the fig tree that immediately shriveled with his curse. Two basic principles come out of these miracles; first, they served people's genuine needs (other than the fig tree incident), and second, each event pointed to Jesus and his authority over things of nature.

Jesus told his disciples that they would do greater works than he had done (John 14:12). They healed others, and Paul escaped from prison through miraculous means (Acts 12:3–19). But many debate today whether the gift still exists, arguing that the miracles of New Testament times were meant to be signs of Jesus's validity as the Son of God, and that numerous times he warned against relying upon continued signs to prove who he was.

But we still say, "Wow, that was a miracle!" Right? Perhaps God nudges some people to step in and be the person who fulfills the miracle for the other person (such as the brother and sister who contacted George Müller). Is it an answer to prayer or a miracle if someone on TikTok hands a struggling mom five hundred dollars in a grocery store? The incident could have been coincidental. Or maybe prayer could be connected: perhaps the struggling mom prayed or maybe the young man felt led by the Holy Spirit.

Someone could participate in the miraculous with a prayerful, listening ear and a heightened sense—even a compulsion—to proceed. The person who is the conduit of God's power in this way might have a strong impression of a need that cannot be otherwise met in a natural sense—with a deep compulsion only brought on by the Spirit of God to follow through with bold and generous action. That person's prayer life may be one that sees work as prayer, stepping in tune with heavenly music designed to bring goodness, grace, and mercy from heaven to earth. And maybe that generous guy on TikTok has a lively prayer life.

## ———— PRAYER POINTERS ————
- Ask God how you can be used by him on earth to meet the needs of others and grow God's kingdom for his glory.
- Look for and record the miraculous in your journal.

## Discernment of Spirits

Some promote a prosperity gospel ("God will make you rich!"). Some promote a gospel of convenience ("You don't need to go to church. Do church wherever you are."). And some promote a gospel that cancels and shapes Scripture to fit the current culture ("Do whatever seems right to you."). Paul saw a similar problem developing in the Corinthian church. There were so-called mystery religions popping up that promoted "mysteries" (1 Cor. 4:1) that would only be revealed to the initiated.[10] But in his writings Paul taught all is now revealed in the person of Jesus Christ; there need be no secrets, no mysteries, no exclusionary societies. With Christ, God revealed his plan: Jesus's incarnation, death, and resurrection, and God's plan of mercy to include all people, no matter their background or former religious experience.

This thinking, commentators say, may explain the inclusion of "distinguishing between spirits" (1 Cor. 12:10), also called *discernment,* as one of the manifestation spiritual gifts. The gift was (and still is) needed to discern between true prophets and false prophets, between good and evil, between that which is from God and that which is from the evil one, and between Christ-following teachers and false teachers simply raising a crowd for their own benefit.

In the Greek the word *discernment* is a clear discrimination, discernment, or distinguishing between that which is evil and that which is good and of God—an ability that leads to and brings about a decision.[11] The Amplified Bible adds this parenthetical explanation: "the ability to distinguish sound, godly doctrine from the deceptive doctrine of man-made religions and cults" (1 Cor. 12:10). Those with this gift would inherently know the answers, as God directed them, to these questions:

- Is it truth?
- Is it biblical?
- Is it from God?

My son-in-law has this gift. He will call someone out by saying, "That's not biblical" or "Jesus would not agree with that." While he loves others well, their opinion of him does not matter; he stands on biblical truth. He has a master of divinity degree, but long before he had letters behind his name, God had given him the ability to differentiate between good spirits and evil ones. His Spanish given name means "God rule." It is appropriate.

He could fit in in Missouri, the Show-Me State; as he and others with the gift of discernment might pray, "Show me, God."

*Direct my steps.*

*Help me see what is right and good and favorable within your will.*

*Distinguish clearly what is evil, so I don't whitewash it, dance around it, and pretend it's all good.*

My son-in-law is tuned in continually to God because we all face an unending stream of choices, and he wants to make the right ones that will advance God's kingdom and cancel the attempts of the enemy. He works in a job that continually encounters deception, and his mind has a laser beam focus that can see through it and say, "No, not today, Satan." May we all have such a gift.

### ─────── PRAYER POINTERS ───────

- Pray for God's discernment of good and evil throughout your day—checking your understanding with God's Word.
- Then ask God for his direction about whether or not to share that understanding.

## Tongues and Interpretation of Tongues

Paul identified two final gifts—"speaking in different kinds of tongues" and "the interpretation of tongues"—in his list in 1 Corinthians 12:4–10. The Greek word for *tongues*, *glossa*, means "languages" or "dialects," but some believe the word includes both earthly and heavenly or ecstatic languages of praise and prayer.[12] The early instances of tongues in Act 2 showed believers speaking in foreign languages others could understand. However, Paul implied the practice changed into one that also included heavenly or ecstatic language directed to God (1 Cor. 14:2). While Paul himself prayed in tongues (v. 18), he implied that public exhibition of this gift might alienate others. And though Paul wrote "where there are tongues, they will be stilled" (1 Cor. 13:8), many today certainly do have the gift and exercise it in their worship.

The gift of interpreting tongues was given to believers for the purpose of translating the language so that hearers could understand. Paul outlined directives that could edify the body.

> The one who prophesies is greater than the one who speaks in tongues, unless someone interprets, so that the church may be edified. (1 Cor. 14:5)

> For this reason the one who speaks in a tongue should pray that they may interpret what they say. (v. 13)

> If anyone speaks in a tongue, two—or at the most three—should speak, one at a time, and someone must interpret. If there is no interpreter, the speaker should keep quiet in the church and speak to himself and God. (vv. 27–28)

The interpreter explains (*diermeneuo* in Greek) what has been spoken, and like all the gifts, interpreting is given for the purpose of building up the body of believers.

Many use this form of praise today as part of their prayer time. Like miracles, it's a sign of faith, as Mark wrote: "In my name they will drive out demons; they will speak in new tongues" (Mark 16:17). So that sign is exercised as a prayerful offering to God—a gift of worship because any ecstatic expression uses a heavenly language only God can understand. The pray-ers are so in tune with the majesty and might of the Lord God that prayer is expressed in ways they could not put together with their own ability. The interpreter clarifies the language of the Holy Spirit for others who are within hearing distance. The Spirit enables the gift of tongues to be expressed (Acts 2:4), and those who have no interpreters may not understand a single word. It simply is a gift meant to share their love and adoration for the Lord God.

## —————————— PRAYER POINTERS ——————————

- Use your gift to express praise to the Father, Son, and Holy Spirit.
- Pray for clarity about how the utterances could be used to edify the body.

Paul wrote that these manifestation gifts are the work of the Holy Spirit, who gives these gifts as he determines. It's our job to simply unwrap the gifts he gives us and put them to use . . . prayerfully.

———— **DISCUSSION QUESTIONS** ————

1. How does someone have the gift of wisdom or knowledge?
2. How would you define the gift of faith—and how would prayer be connected to this gift?
3. How would those with the gift of healing pray?
4. How could we participate with God in the miraculous through prayer?
5. What's the difference between normal discernment and the gift of discernment of spirits?
6. How is speaking in tongues a form of prayer?
7. Do any of the Prayer Pointers appeal to you? Which ones and why?

*Chapter 15*

# Motivational Gifts

WE ARE ALL MEMBERS, PAUL wrote, of one body, the church. While today we think of the word *member* relating to a member of Congress or a member of an organization, the origin of the word *member* (*melos* in Greek) related to a limb of the body. Paul's metaphor means that each person is essential for full function of the figurative body of Christ, and each must work together for unity and harmony of operation. Each member is no more vital than another.[1] Eugene Peterson expresses this well in *The Message* paraphrase:

> The way God designed our bodies is a model for understanding our lives together as a church: every part dependent on every other part, the parts we mention and the parts we don't, the parts we see and the parts we don't. If one part hurts, every other part is involved in the hurt, and in the healing. If one part flourishes, every other part enters into the exuberance.
>
> You are Christ's body—that's who you are! You must never forget this. Only as you accept your part of that body does your "part" mean anything. (1 Cor. 12:25–27)

I mention this before we examine several spiritual gifts that may not seem as flashy or as public as others. These are the motivational gifts—those that come from your motivation to see others spurred to action. If you have these gifts, you take action and want to spur others to action as well.

## Service

"Put me to work," my friend said. "I need to do something."

While I thought I would have everything under control for the conference, I was behind in getting things set up. Usually I would have said, "No, it's okay. Just sit down and enjoy yourself." However, with a quick glance at the clock, I said, "Sure," and pointed her to the table decorations. In no time, she had the tables looking beautiful—better than I could have done.

The Greek word for *service* is *diakonia*, "the office and work of a *diakonos*" in service of the Christian believers. Do you see the connection with the word *deacon* here? The *diakonos*, or deacon, would attend to the needs of believers. The original word implies a connection to the *work* of the church, as opposed to a connection to a master or owner (like a bondservant or slave). The verb form gives us a picture of someone hastening after or pursuing the work—with the origin of the word relating to a runner. Those of us with the gift of service take joy in being a runner for the good of the Christian body. Devotion and love are related to all exercising their spiritual gifts: "Be devoted to one another in love. Honor one another above yourselves. Never be lacking in zeal, but keep your spiritual fervor, serving the Lord" (Rom. 12:10–11). When we serve others, love unifies us all.

Those with the gift of service have eyes wide open for needs around them, interceding as their days pass. Just as they step in to serve where help is needed—perhaps even instinctively without being asked—they step into prayer. Many say they pray throughout their day, but those with this gift of service truly do. In the same way they want to see needs fulfilled, they also serve others through prayer.

The writer James was a do-er who emphasized the importance of works to provide evidence of one's faith. I think those with the gift of service would nod their heads at some of the final words in his letter to the twelve tribes:

> Is anyone among you in trouble? Let them pray. Is anyone happy? Let them sing songs of praise. Is anyone among you sick? Let them call the elders of the church to pray over them and anoint them with oil in the name of the Lord. And the prayer offered in faith will make the sick person well; the Lord will raise them up. If he has sinned, they will be forgiven. Therefore confess your sins to each other and pray for each other so that you may be healed. The prayer of a righteous person is powerful and effective. (James 5:13–16)

Prayer is problem-solving. We serve with prayer as we lift up the needs around us.

## PRAYER POINTERS

- Keep your prayer radar up. Pray as you serve. And don't worry about waiting to be asked to serve. Just step in prayerfully to fill the needs you see.
- View prayer as a form of service too. Volunteer for your church and other prayer chains and lift up needs as you learn of them.

## Exhortation

"I've been praying for you," my writing coach said, "and I really sense you should write an online course on prayer."

"Okay . . ." I said, feeling somewhat overwhelmed.

"And you could call it Prayer School."

That idea clung to me for the next several months. Her confidence in me encouraged me to jump in and put together modules and lessons that God had been teaching me for more than twenty years as I had been combing the Bible and classic writings in my figurative School of Prayer. Alice exercised her spiritual gift of encouragement (or exhortation) to push me to a ministry form I had not yet considered.

Another of the motivational gifts is encouragement, and Paul wrote, "if it is to encourage, then give encouragement" (Rom. 12:8). The Greek word is *parakalon* (exhorting) (the noun is *paraklesei*), which means "to stimulate, beseech, exhort, comfort, encourage, advocate, or entreaty."[2] We see the same word used several times in Acts:

> When [Barnabas] arrived [in Antioch] and saw what the grace of God had done, he was glad and *encouraged* them all to remain true to the Lord with all their hearts. (Acts 11:23, emphasis added)

> After the reading from the Law and the Prophets, the leaders of the synagogue sent word to them, saying, "Brothers, if you have a word of *exhortation* for the people, please speak." (Acts 13:15, emphasis added)

> Judas and Silas, who themselves were prophets, said much to *encourage* and strengthen the believers. (Acts 15:32, emphasis added)

The idea of *encouragement* used here is stronger than our usual connotation today, encompassing the work of exhortation as well. Exhortation (*paraklesei*) would nudge someone to action and completion of ministry. The prefix *para-* means "beside" or "alongside of," something we see in the verses above. Barnabas wasn't merely patting new believers on the back; he came alongside them and urged them to remain true—to live out their faith. When the synagogue rulers asked Paul and the others for a message of encouragement, Paul proceeded into a long discourse. Encouragement from Judas and Silas strengthened the believers in Antioch. These exhortational expressions were more than compliments; they were words of teaching and coaching that built up the body.

Those with the gift of exhortation have a passion for moving the kingdom message forward. They read the Bible purposefully, pray intently, listen in prayer for the Lord's application, and then encourage and exhort others to action. They have quiet confidence that only arises from long sessions seeking God's word for others, patiently and quietly listening for the Lord to speak. It was only because Alice had sought the Lord's words for me that she could sweetly yet boldly encourage me to take the next steps God had ordained for me.

### PRAYER POINTERS

- Seek the heart of God for those around you. Ask what he sees in those people.
- Share God's love with others and pray with them.

## Giving

When I served on the board of trustees at our church a few years ago, the church received an anonymous gift of more than one million dollars, with no caveat about how to use it. At this writing, construction was just completed on a new welcome center that connects our eighty-year-old sanctuary building with the educational and activities center. I was privileged to vote with the other board members to approve that project, something the general church body did as well—matching the funds to make the best use of the gift.

God gifts some believers with the spiritual gift of generosity. They see a need and open their wallets to give. In his Romans 12 list of spiritual gifts, Paul wrote, "if it is giving, then give generously" (v. 8, one version uses the word *liberality*). One need not be rich to have this gift. Jesus taught this in observation of the widow's mite:

> As Jesus looked up, he saw the rich putting their gifts into the temple treasury. He also saw a poor widow put in two very small copper coins. "Truly I tell you," he said, "this poor widow has put in more than all the others. All these people gave their gifts out of their wealth; but she out of her poverty put in all she had to live on." (Luke 21:1–4)

The widow was poor but gave all she had. Her very small gift was more important than the larger tithes of those who had more. The gift of giving does not necessarily imply someone with the gift will be rich.

The Greek word for giving, *metadidous*, implies a change of ownership. As with the donation I mentioned, the gift is simply handed over with no expectations of how it might be used for ministry. Paul used the people of the church in Macedonia as examples of generous giving:

- They gave with overflowing joy, despite severe trials (2 Cor. 8:2).
- They gave even out of their extreme poverty (v. 2).
- They gave beyond their ability (v. 3).
- They saw giving as a privilege and even pleaded for the opportunity to give (v. 4).
- Their gift was unexpected—not given out of obligation or tithe (v. 5).

A key to this gift is seen in this expression from Paul: "They gave themselves first of all to the Lord, and then by the will of God also to us" (v. 5). Those with the gift of giving respond to the Lord's leading without needing to know the circumstances or having a need for approval or payback of any kind.

Earlier we looked briefly at the prayer life of George Müller, who had the spiritual gift of faith; he prayed to God as needs for his orphanages arose, and others fulfilled those needs with their giving—without ever having heard from him. Let's now think of those on the other end of that giving—those who responded to those prayers not by knowing the need but by being so close to the Father, Son, and Holy Spirit that they felt godly nudges to give. Those with the spiritual gift of giving—those who actually follow through and do give—may see a need and give with God's leading or may simply respond to God's direction without knowing any kind of proposed outcome.

These praying folks may have lots of prayer closet time when they hear God's voice, and they may also have the gift of knowledge and know, deep in their hearts, that the funds they have belong to ministry or someone else in need. I don't know how to explain the times when I drive by a panhandler without handing over dollars, as opposed to when I sense God wants me to give a certain amount. Perhaps the difference *is* prayer; maybe in the former, my mind is elsewhere, whereas in the latter I've been talking with God. In any case, those with a giving gift see others with the Lord's eyes and respond. Prayer can be expressed kinesthetically; giving is a prayerful act.

## PRAYER POINTERS

- Pray as you hear of needs, seeking God's direction for giving. Not every need requires a gift.
- Pray for the recipients, that they would pursue a personal relationship with Christ. Keep them in prayer in the days ahead.

## Leadership

I never had to choose leaders when I divided my classes into groups. I would just say, "Leaders, you know who you are. Lead." Almost instantly they would speak up, accept their role, and provide direction for the group. Leaders take the lead. They step up, assume responsibility, and get the job done.

We will find the same true for the spiritual gift of leadership. Paul wrote in Romans 12:8, "if [the spiritual gift] is to lead, do it diligently." I almost overlooked an important word in that statement: *do*. Leaders will automatically jump into leadership and get things in motion. They provide direction and answer many questions that a community of believers will have—be that a church, a parachurch ministry, a Christian nonprofit, or even a small group. *What do we do now? How will we do it? When and where will we do it? Who will do what?* And so on. They may be leading alongside other leaders with various kinds of giftings and talents—administration, evangelism, pastoring, wisdom, teaching, encouragement, knowledge—and they may have several of those gifts themselves. However, those with the gift of leadership are not necessarily good at administration or some of those other gifts. Leaders provide direction for others.

One commentary says Paul may have been referring to the concept of elders with the Romans 12:8 mention of leadership.[3] The Ephesian church had elders by the time his letter to the Romans was written, and we read in Acts 20:17–38 that Paul shared his plans with that church and prayed with them. He also encouraged the Thessalonians to respect "those who work hard among you, who care for you in the Lord and who admonish you" (1 Thess. 5:12)—a probable reference to elders. And Paul wrote to Timothy that elders who direct the affairs of the church are worthy of double honor, especially those whose work is preaching and teaching (1 Tim. 5:17). From these references we learn that leaders work hard and guide others as they orchestrate the church's affairs under the Lord's direction.

Leaders like to see plans come to fruition. While they might be inclined to forge ahead with their own seemingly great ideas, slowing down prayerfully will help them be "in the Lord," as Paul wrote, and envision not their own plans but God's. Paul was a leader, and we know that Paul prayed a lot for both individuals and churches. Those prayers demonstrated his passion for the spread of the gospel and for maturation of those who had come to know Christ. He may not have journaled, but he did write out prayers in his letters. Slowing down to write out prayers could be a methodology for those with the gift of leadership to spend more time in prayer through the use of pen and paper. And they might eventually resonate with Jesus's Gethsemane prayer: *Thy will be done.*

─────────── **PRAYER POINTERS** ───────────

- Get a posse of praying people alongside you who will pray for and with you as you minister to others.
- Set aside daily time for scheduled prayer: the busier your schedule, the more time in prayer is needed.

## Administration

A few years ago Craig and I had the opportunity to visit Hawaii to watch our youngest receive her master's degree at the University of Hawaii. Afterward we three took a few days away to Kauai, where we toured that island and experienced a fabulous dinner cruise along the Na Pali coast. The ship's pilot challenged us to stand at the very front of the boat—the bow pulpit—to touch a waterfall coming off a cliff. Slowly he steered the boat toward the waterfall until—splash!—he manipulated a good shower for us. Stepping back away gave us perspective about how expert the pilot was to move so close to the cliff and yet not touch it.

I mention this vignette because the Greek word for pilot is *kybernesis*. The literal meaning has to do with steering or pilotage, but Paul employs a metaphorical use of the word in 1 Corinthians 12:28:

"And God has appointed these in the church: . . . administrations" (NKJV) Paul uses *kybernesis* here for what is translated *administration*— the only time that Greek word is used in Scripture.[4] Those who pilot churches steer those Christian bodies. They guide them through storms and narrow, potentially dangerous places and make sure they are following the Master Pilot, Christ. The Holy Spirit enables those with the spiritual gift of administration to carry out and organize plans and spiritual programs in the church. Administrators are good at breaking down ministry goals into action plans, delegating responsibilities, and making sure all the details are carried out. They are good at recognizing gifts and talents in others and calling upon them to utilize those strengths for the sake of the church's mission.

Because administrators are detail-oriented and excel at systems, flow charts, and spreadsheet-and-Google-docs everything, people with this gift might find two particular prayer systems effective. The first is a numbered prayer list they could keep in a journal or even online. The second is a notebook with sections that organize the days of the week into different kinds of prayer focuses. Administrative pray-ers might find great satisfaction in setting up a checklist for those various targeted areas, as they probably find joy in organizing things and checking them off when God provides the answers. They would be faithful to such systems and James's call:

Is anyone among you in trouble? Let them pray. Is anyone happy? Let them sing songs of praise. Is anyone among you sick? Let them call the elders of the church to pray over them and anoint them with oil in the name of the Lord. And the prayer offered in faith will make the sick person well; the Lord will raise them up. If they have sinned, they will be forgiven. Therefore confess your sins to each other and pray for each other so that you may be healed. The prayer of a righteous person is powerful and effective.

Elijah was a human being, even as we are. He prayed earnestly that it would not rain, and it did not rain on the land for three and a half years. Again he prayed, and the heavens gave rain, and the earth produced its crops. (James 5:13–18)

James shows us here several ways to pray—petitions (prayers for ourselves), praise, intercession (prayers for others), confession. Richard Foster suggests twenty-one different kinds of prayers in his book *Prayer: Finding the Heart's True Home,* adding to the above simple prayer, prayer of the forsaken, prayer of tears, prayer of relinquishment, and many others.[5] Those with the gift of administration likely prefer having days organized into strategies, and praying differently on different days of the week might be an appealing methodology.

## PRAYER POINTERS

- Organize prayer needs into a notebook or other system that makes sense for you. The National Day of Prayer Task Force has seven areas of prayer that make sense for a weekly routine: family, church, business, education, military, government, and arts/entertainment/media.
- Pray daily that God will direct your plans.

## Mercy

Undoubtedly, you've seen the last spiritual gift, mercy, extended in many quiet ways. Perhaps a family member faithfully took care of an aging loved one. Or you have a friend who always visits church members in the hospital and takes meals to sick folks at home. Paul wrote, "if it is to show mercy, do it cheerfully" (Rom. 12:8). For those with the gift of mercy, that reminder was probably not necessary, as they "mourn with those who mourn" (v. 15) and take seriously the responsibility to "carry each other's burdens" (Gal. 6:2). Showing mercy is something that blesses not only the receiver but also the giver.

The translated term *showing mercy* best represents the gift. The Greek word *eleeo* is a verb: one not only feels sympathy with the misery of another; he acts on that sentiment.[6] So the gift really isn't mercy—it's *demonstrating* mercy, an outward manifestation of compassion. We find the term in a couple further mentions from Paul that indicate the motivation and purpose for this gift:

> Even though I was once a blasphemer and a persecutor and a violent man, I was *shown mercy* because I acted in ignorance and unbelief. (1 Tim. 1:13, emphasis added)

> But for that very reason I was *shown mercy* so that in me, the worst of sinners, Christ Jesus might display his immense patience as an example for those who would believe in him and receive eternal life. (v. 16, emphasis added)

The underlying motivation for showing mercy is an internalized knowledge that Jesus has shown mercy to us, and the purpose of the gift is to point others to him so that they, too, can experience his saving grace.

Mercy givers are good listeners, so this naturally becomes part of their daily prayer time. They are the figurative hands and feet of the Healer, Jesus, and bring comfort and care that aids in others' healing process. They pray often and long—faithful to requests to intercede quietly, listening for the Lord's direction to provide patient care for those who are suffering. With the Spirit's strength, they represent the body of Christ to others going through tough circumstances. They see with the eyes of Christ, hear with the ears of Christ, speak his words, and offer loving care in the same way that Jesus did on this earth.

I read a short story on Facebook of a little boy who saw a homeless man sleeping on the street and left his mother's grip to ask the man if he was all right. The man said he was homeless—that he had lost his home and a family member to a fire and had nothing left. The little boy gave him the couple dollars he had in his pocket and then persuaded his mother to give him more. Others watching also helped the man. That little boy showed mercy in the same way Jesus did to all the afflicted he encountered. I wonder, if we prayed for this gift, if God would indeed bless us with his eyes and ears and heart.

―――――――――― **PRAYER POINTERS** ――――――――――

- Pray about how you could be the figurative hands and feet of Jesus to someone in need on your prayer list.
- Ask God how doing something might be a prayerful response as God brings someone to mind.

―――――――――― **DISCUSSION QUESTIONS** ――――――――――

1. Earlier we learned that Joshua responded prayerfully through obedience. How does what he did relate to the spiritual gift of service?
2. How is the gift of exhortation connected to prayer?
3. The author writes, "The Greek word for giving, *metadidous*, implies a change of ownership." How is a prayerful posture also a change of ownership?
4. How did the church in Macedonia demonstrate the gift of giving? How might prayer have something to do with this gift?
5. How is prayer connected to the spiritual gifts of leadership and administration?
6. Those with the gift of mercy not only *feel* sympathy for others; they act on it. Who do you know who has this gift, and how does that person use the gift?
7. Do any of the Prayer Pointers appeal to you? Which ones and why?

# PART FOUR

## Your Praying Style

*Chapter 16*

# Finding Your Praying Style

THROUGHOUT THIS BOOK I'VE OFFERED reference points to help you better understand your God-given personality, natural tendencies, and spiritual giftings—including an examination of people in the Bible and how they prayed. As I've written earlier, the trickiest part of taking any personality assessment is being objective about who we are.

Years ago when I had young kids, I saw myself as someone with a melancholy personality, because I was depressed much of the time. As the years have passed, though, I've grown in understanding that I lean more toward the strong-minded choleric personality who more easily slips into anger than depression.

As you have probably already found, the Praying Personality Quiz is in this book's appendix. Please take it now, being as objective about yourself as possible—remembering that some of us are those forceful lions as opposed to the fun-loving otters we all might like to be. And it's possible that your generational and family background—including church and spiritual practices in the home—have influenced your perception of what seems natural in regard to prayer. Here are some suggestions as you approach the quiz:

- Don't overthink it. Go with the answer that seems *most* like you.
- Where are you currently? Don't think about the sum of your past. Don't think about what you would *like* to be. Who are you now?
- Remember that this is not a judgment call. No one but you will see your results. One praying style is not better than another.
- In other words, choose the answer that is right for you. There is no best answer. We can all get A's on this test . . . especially if we're being objective about who we are.
- Consider how others might answer the test for you. Sometimes others see us better than we do ourselves.

After you've taken the test, come back to this chapter to see if the personality that scored the most points meshes with the description that follows below. But make sure you do read the whole chapter. Another praying style might make sense for your lifestyle. As with other personality tests, determining praying personalities is not a science but is instead based on observation, study, and insights from God's Word. And no matter your personality, read through to the last section called "Bottom Line," which is for all of us.

Before writing this book, I thought there might be a dozen or more different kinds of praying styles. However, as I've immersed myself into the various personality assessments, as well as the study of praying biblical characters and spiritual gifts, I've discovered that there seem to be just four classic kinds of praying folks.

## The Problem Solver

The Problem Solvers see prayer as a problem-solving strategy. They like quick answers to problems and know that our heavenly Father is the best one to run to when life presents struggles—not only for themselves but also for others. Because they're good at making decisions, early in their faith journey they may struggle with handing things over to God. In fact, they love solving their own problems and can often find themselves mentally solving others' problems as they are in conversation with them. But as Problem Solvers mature in Christ, they understand that handing over needs to the Lord in prayer ultimately leads to the desirable end result.

Problem Solvers study the Bible for answers, and they understand God speaks to them daily in its pages. In fact, they find inspiration in the Word for their prayers, as it provides authority behind them. They do not let questions about the faith bog them down but instead search the Bible for the answers they need and trust God.

When problems arise, they immediately send their to-the-point prayer requests to trusted friends and prayer groups. Their prayers are big, bold, and full of faith. They believe God can do the impossible and are not afraid to ask him to do just that. When they get others' prayer requests, they pray right then and there, because they like checking things off their mental lists. And when someone shares a need in person, the Problem Solvers might say, "Let me pray for you right now," and they do so confidently. In groups they are focused, tend to plan their spoken prayers, and pray purposefully and succinctly. Problem Solvers love to hear answers to their prayers—there's just a certain personal satisfaction to all that. However, when they do not get the answers they want, they can get frustrated because of a personality bent toward wanting to control a situation.

Their own prayer times tend to be short and sweet—and often on the go, like in the car. They can meditate prayerfully on a Scripture verse, but that time would probably be short. They like to prayerwalk, because they can get two things done at the same time—exercise and intercession for their neighbors and those on their hearts. They struggle with slowing down because there's always something more to do. But when Problem Solvers learn that the Lord wants them to seek his presence, not just his answers, they will make extended prayer time a priority.

──────── **PRAYER POINTERS** ────────

- Prayerwalking: There are two schools of thought on this practice. Some take their mental prayer lists for family members, friends, jobs, and personal struggles to the street. I call that "walking and praying." Those in prayer networks, though, see prayerwalking as an intercessory practice. You pray for what you see—interceding for the needs of those in homes you pass, business owners, staff in schools, commuters and others driving by, and so on. You open up your eyes, take a focused look around you, and pray as you go. What will thrill the Problem Solvers is they will begin to observe answers to prayer . . . and remember, they just love checking things off their mental list!

- Exercising prayer: Similarly, some may prefer to have their prayer time as they work out on a treadmill or other workout equipment. They will want to remember to wear a noise-reducing headset, though, so they can focus on prayer rather than the surroundings.

- Posting prayer reminders: The Problem Solvers probably don't want to take time for creating prayers lists or writing out prayers in a journal. But they appreciate reminders. They may post sticky notes on the fridge or on a bathroom mirror. They might purposefully make a photo display on a bulletin board depicting loved ones as prompts to pray for them. A "Pray Big" sign could be a reminder to pray for long-term prayer concerns. Even decorative objects could inspire prayer: a friend just gave me a handmade pottery bowl I will use as a prayer bowl that will hold sticky notes with prayer requests on them.

- Fasting: Giving up food for a certain length of time would help the Problem Solver remember to pray for problematic issues that need breakthrough. Jesus said, "When you fast . . ." not "If you fast . . ." and Problem Solvers follow biblical direction.

- Organizing prayer chains: Problem Solvers are natural leaders who take charge of ministry-related programs. Volunteering to lead the church's or another group's prayer chain (via email or texting) can put them in a position to know of prayer needs, pray, and get them disseminated efficiently to intercessors. They will be quickly responsive and appreciated.

## The Friend of God

As the name implies, the Friend of God views the Lord as a companion and friend, so these folks go to prayer when they need God's fellowship, closeness, affection, and intimacy. Their prayers resemble conversation, and they sense God's participation in that exchange. Friends of God are passionate about prayer, particularly when it involves others because they are outgoing and socially minded; they prefer being with people more than being alone. Friends of God have a running conversation with God throughout the day—on the go, whenever and wherever—rather than a sit-down, be-quiet practice.

They love the Bible because it has characters with stories that inspire their prayers, and they lovingly trust God, rarely questioning his answers to their prayers. Instead, they might feel hurt, as though a friend let them down. They might also sense God speaking to them through friends and family, so when a challenge arises, they call them, talk for a length of time, and entrust them with their prayer requests.

Prayer time with others feeds Friends of God and gives them life-giving energy and a positive outlook. They connect easily with people and love sharing their stories of God's answers to prayer. In a circle of praying friends, they provide spontaneous, personal, cheerful prayers that encourage others. Prayer with others is definitely a comfort zone for the Friends of God—especially like-minded family—and when they hear of answers to prayer, they call that person to celebrate.

Prayers for themselves are not necessarily part of the routine for Friends of God. They live to surround themselves with others and love them well, and so their prayers will focus on those they love. Because they are high energy and extroverted, meditation would probably not be part of their routine.

————— **PRAYER POINTERS** —————

- Worshipping: Friends of God find that worship music provides an atmosphere for prayer. Their prayer time is spent singing or humming along. Even if alone, these extroverts will feel as though someone is with them.
- Praying with others: These fun-loving friends need their family, friends, and others around them to pray. It's a social, relational event that helps them connect with others and develop their relationship with God.
- On-the-go praying: With children in the car headed for a ball game or music lessons, it's a perfect setting for the Friend of God to pray with her kids, which models and teaches them how to pray—a double benefit. Spontaneous prayer is this person's mode of operation, as opposed to weekly, scheduled meetings.
- Phoning a friend: When in crisis, the Friend of God will naturally turn to a friend for prayer support. It's important to ask that friend to pray with you specifically, as opposed to praying later alone.

## The Organized Pray-er

Organized Pray-ers have systems and routines for prayer. They use planners, journals, and guides, and they make prayer part of their daily schedule. These people have a prayer closet—a literal one or a specially designated place where their Bible and prayer materials are perfectly organized and ready for them to use.

They deeply feel compassion for others going through crises and take to heart requests from others to pray, writing down the request in a notebook or journal, dating it, and praying faithfully until an answer is reached. The Organized Pray-ers pray for themselves a lot—and a summation of these prayers might be this: "Help!" Meditation will lift their spirits, and so they make time in their schedule for long intervals of quiet time. Prayer is a serious matter for the Organized Pray-er, who also goes to prayer at other times when she is discouraged or sad. Another name for the Organized Pray-ers could be The Lamenters, because they feel deeply.

Organized Pray-ers read the Bible in a systematic way because it helps them know they are not alone and because they often have unsettled questions about the faith. Their prayers often reflect their mood, and so the biblical laments and other poetic literature are particularly appealing to this personality.

Praying with a group is challenging for this introverted person, who would prefer to be by herself. She's reluctant to share her own prayer needs, but she will listen with empathy and pray along silently. If someone asks her to pray, she might get emotional in such a public setting, but she'll continue to pray later for that person and might even send a personal note expressing her love and concern. Prayers that are not answered in the way the Organized Pray-er requested would make them sad, and those thoughts might overshadow their outlook for a period of time.

## ——— PRAYER POINTERS ———

- Prayer listing: They might use a comprehensive journal with all the prayer requests dated and updated—a popular alternative being the bullet journal. Others might utilize an organized notebook of prayer requests, divided into sections for days of the week. For example, Sundays they pray for family, Mondays for friends, etc. Another method could be a phone app or the notes function to track prayer requests.
- Creating prayer art: Organized Pray-ers are often artistic in nature and love the idea of creating while praying. The artwork might actually be their expression of prayer. They might draw or paint or color creative Bible journaling pages while praying,

because their highest expression of prayer is to imitate the Creator.

- Writing out prayers: This person could also journal her prayers. She doesn't just say them quietly: she writes them out. She might even find inspiration from the Bible and turn Scripture into prayers that she creates.
- Prayer closet praying: The Organized Pray-er needs a special, organized place to settle into prayer, such as a literal prayer closet (some empty a closet and create a reflection place) or a reserved spot in a bedroom or living room with just the right lighting, comfy seating, and a basket or shelf ready with a Bible and other materials. In that cozy or inspirational spot, she can pray for long periods of time.
- Poetic praying: This praying person could also express herself by writing poetic prayers.
- Labyrinth praying: This pray-er might find a labyrinth-type experience meaningful. This person slowly walks alone toward the center of the labyrinth with confession, thanksgiving, and praise as an offering, and then out of the labyrinth listening to God for his presence and guidance. This can also be done on a high school track with certain numbers of laps to mark the stages of prayer.

## The Peace Seeker

The primary reason this personality goes to prayer is to seek and find peace. Peace Seekers naturally go to prayer when there is chaos and confusion. If everything is going smoothly, prayer might not be on their natural radar. They know, though, that prayer is the best place to go—even if it might not be their first response. It just takes them a while to get there. However, when they do establish a convenient routine for prayer, they are faithful to it.

Peace Seekers' prayers are informal and sometimes include questions. They're always striving for an even, routine, peaceful life, so they find meditation helpful to get to that personal place. Peace Seekers find that the Bible is a good resource when they don't know how to pray. Confusion and questions may arise if their prayers are not answered in the way they desired, but they will patiently wait out the situation to see how God will redeem it. When prayers are answered as they hoped, they thank God quietly rather than make a big hoopla.

In groups of praying folks, they listen intently, pray silently, and probably won't offer to pray unless encouraged to do so. Peace Seekers may not pray much for themselves, but they do care about others and their needs, and when they commit to praying for someone, they are steadfast.

## —— PRAYER POINTERS ——

- Utilizing prayer books: Peace Seekers might not create their own system for praying, but they would find a book of prayers helpful to guide their own. Once they're in a routine, they will follow the prescribed plan.
- Using prayer apps: There are many apps people can add to their cell phones that provide prompts for prayer or a prayer for the day. Having these pop up daily will help this personality stay on a regular routine.
- Enjoying God with coffee: Peace Seekers thrive on routines, like those habits that fall into place every morning. A good time for prayer might be with that first cup of coffee, providing a slow, easy yet effective start to the day.
- Praying a formula: There are several mnemonics that can remind these folks to pray. With each letter of the acronym, the Peace Seeker can be prompted to pray in that vein.

    ACTS: adoration, confession, thanksgiving, supplication

    PRAY: praise God, reveal need, adoration, and *yes* to God (thanksgiving)

    TRIP: thanksgiving, regret, intercession, purpose/plan

PARTS: praise, ask, repent, thanks, share (Who should I talk to?)

5 fingers: You can use your five fingers as reminders, creating your own system or one like this:

- Thumb: Confess your sins.
- Index finger: Give thanks.
- Middle finger: Offer praise.
- Ring finger: Pray for others.
- Little finger: Pray for yourself.

## Bottom Line

This book was never meant to give anyone a Get-Out-of-Prayer Card. It's human nature to skip, gloss over, or rush spiritual disciplines. They aren't screaming at us as our schedules and appointments do or pushing us as our family and jobs do. The truth is most of us don't like *tarrying*. No matter the personality, we don't like putting our world on hold while dialing in to Jesus. But let's look at what he said about tarrying.

After Jesus left the upper room—where he washed the disciples' feet and led them in the Last Supper; where Peter said he would never deny him and Jesus taught them about the Vine and branches; and where Judas decided to betray him—Jesus went to prayer. First, he prayed in the upper room, and then he went to the garden at Gethsemane. There he asked his disciples to keep watch while he prayed. At least three of the disciples were there—Peter, James, and John. All of them dozed off. Even after Jesus roused them and reminded them twice, they repeated the same behavior. Here's what happened:

> When he came back to his disciples, he found them sound asleep. He said to Peter, "Can't you stick it out with me a single hour? Stay alert; be in prayer so you don't wander into temptation without even knowing you're in danger. There is a part of you that is eager, ready for anything in God. But there's

another part that's as lazy as an old dog sleeping by the fire."
(Matt. 26:40–41 MSG)

The disciples couldn't tarry with Jesus in the most critical hour of his life up until then. They knew the authorities were after him. Gethsemane was just a gully away from the walled city of Jerusalem, just minutes' walking distance from the temple. Until I saw it for myself in the fall of 2018, I always thought this Gethsemane scene and the crucifixion were on hills far away, but no, they're about a mile apart. Easy pickings for the enemies of Jesus seeking his arrest.

Years ago I read a book that challenged and then changed me: *Could You Not Tarry One Hour?* by Larry Lea. As a working mom of four kids at the time, an hour of prayer seemed impossible. It was too much to ask—the author suggesting I pray that much. But then because of a physical breakdown, I started prayerwalking early in the morning and found that an hour passed easily as I prayed for the businesses, schools, churches, government offices, and anything else in my eyes' pathway. I can recall the precise moment when I stepped off a curb to cross a small street and realized I couldn't get everything prayed for in an hour. There were so many needs that I felt compelled to keep going. And then it hit me: *Oh . . . just stay in prayer through the rest of the day.* I began to understand that wherever I am, there's a need for prayer.

My tarrying in prayer led to a praying-without-ceasing lifestyle. I don't mean for that to sound spiritually arrogant. But my eyesight—my mindset—switched as I began to understand the joy of spending time with the Lord through prayer. It's no longer a duty, an obligation, a simple line item in my bullet journal, but instead, it's a deep desire to take advantage of the privilege the Lord God offers me—his presence.

I am still an on-the-go pray-er. It's still hard for me to sit still for even five minutes to pray. I want to get two things done at once—an extra task crossed off my list *while* I take care of prayer. But a few years ago I bought myself a prayer chair—a comfortable chair with an ottoman in my office where I can go for a prayer break. It takes me away from my mental lists and prayer stickies and that ever-shouting calendar to experience the best time of my day: sitting with God. I pray with open hands and heart and mind, offering myself to him and then waiting for what he may have for me.

Sometimes those received blessings are new ideas. Sometimes they're responses and guidance for my "pray BIG" prayers. Sometimes they're promptings to pray for others. And sometimes they're simple affirmation of God's love for me. Ultimately, though, the best reason to pray is that we simply want to be with God. A young woman I know says of her husband, "He's my favorite person." And that's how I see the Lord God—through the person of Jesus Christ, God in flesh. He's my favorite Person. And I like tarrying with him.

The Puritan writer Richard Baxter puts this perfectly:

> Make it your business in every duty to wind up your affections nearer heaven. What we receive from God is answerable to our own desires and ends. Do not come to your duties with any lower ends. Renounce formality, custom, and applause. When you kneel in secret or public prayer, let it be in hope to get your heart nearer God before you rise. When you open your Bible or other books, let it be with the hope of finding some passage of divine truth and some such blessing of the Spirit with it that may raise your affections nearer heaven and give you a fuller taste of it. When you step out your door on the way to church, say to yourself, "I hope to meet with something from God that may raise my affections before I return. I hope the Spirit will sweeten my heart with celestial delights. I hope that Christ will shine about me with light from heaven, let me hear his instructing and reviving voice, and cause the scales to fall from my eyes, so that I may see more of that glory than I ever saw before (Acts 9:3–4, 18)." If these were our ends and

this our course when we set about our duty, we would not be as strange to heaven as we are.[1]

Prayer points us to heaven. Prayer gets us looking up. Prayer whisks worries and anxieties away. You see, prayer gives us perspective about what is awful and what is heaven-sent. Heaven looks sweeter to the praying person and allows us to align our hearts more closely with God's heart. That means we not only delight in him but also delight in the circumstances he allows into our lives. Prayer begins to set a glow inside of us that others find inviting, even curious . . . so much so that they ask, "What's different about you, this glowy thing you have?" So prayer not only draws us more closely to our Creator but also draws others, through us, to him as well.

And that, my friend, makes prayer worth the tarrying.

## ——— DISCUSSION QUESTIONS ———

1. What were your results of the Praying Personalities Quiz? How do you feel about the results?
2. As you read each of the descriptions of the four Praying Personalities, which seem to resonate with you the most?
3. If you've taken personality assessments in the past, do the results from the Praying Personalities Quiz make sense as you connect them with those other assessments?
4. What are your prayer strengths, do you think? What are any weak points you see from your prayer life?
5. What kinds of praying practices seem to be the most natural for you?
6. Summarize the author's comments in the Bottom Line section of the chapter. What are your reactions to these thoughts?
7. What have you learned from this book about yourself and prayer? How might your prayer life deepen as a result of what you've learned?

# Acknowledgments

THE IDEA FOR THIS BOOK first gelled when I was speaking to a group of writers called the She Writes for Him Tribe, for which I am now the community manager. I had been asked to speak about how writers can incorporate more prayer into their lives, and so I listed dozens of ways to do just that. Toward the end of my presentation, I said something like, "Maybe it has something to do with our God-given personalities. Perhaps there are praying personalities."

There was a moment of silence. And then I said, "Wow, I think that's a book."

Less than a year later, the kind folks at Kregel Publications thought so too. I am very thankful to Jerry Kregel, Catherine DeVries, Janyre Tromp, Rachel Kirsch, and Lindsay Danielson, who have supported this book and pulled the best out of me. You won my heart when you put my name on the welcome sign outside Kregel offices in Grand Rapids. I am also appreciative of the terrific editorial help from Tisha Martin, Amy Tol, and Robert Ludkey—you are excellent.

I also greatly appreciate the direction and friendship of my agent, Janet Grant, of Books & Such Literary Management. I think this may be the first book idea of mine she completely loved from the get-go. Janet, your guidance over more than thirty years of doing books together has been invaluable.

Two experts in personality were particularly helpful. Linda Goldfarb has been a tremendous resource and encouragement to me as I crafted the Praying Personalities Quiz. She and Linda Gilden are the authors of the LINKED® Quick Guide to Personalities books, and I recommend those books highly. Many thanks to them as they coached me through personalities training certification—I was not the easiest of students to handle! Many thanks also to my friend Lori Young, a Christian trained in the use of the Enneagram, who helped me hone the scenarios I created.

I am blessed with many praying friends. Two I can text at any time: Kim West and Maggie Folkers. Thank you, friends, for your constant love and care for me prayer-wise and otherwise. And a group hug of appreciation to my Advanced Writers and Speakers Association mastermind group: thank you!

My husband, Craig, has always been a huge supporter of my writing. He took care of four kids when I tromped off to writers' conferences, and he is still my Yes Man when I ask him to take me to the airport at 3 a.m. I love you, Craig, and I probably owe you a couple more pies.

Lastly, but most importantly, I thank my Lord Jesus, for helping me write a book that was beyond my reach. May this draw others to a closer relationship with you, my Advocate and Redeemer of any and all my mistakes, writing-wise or otherwise.

*Appendix*

# Praying Personality Quiz

THE PRAYING PERSONALITY QUIZ CAN be a helpful tool to find or confirm your praying personality. The directions and suggestions are simple:

- Circle the one answer that seems most like you. Though you may feel more than one answer applies to you, go with the one that is more like you than any other.
- Consider how you are now, as opposed to what you have been in the past or what you *hope* to be in the future.
- Think about what others who know you best might say about you.
- Don't overthink or dwell on answers too long. Your first hunch is probably the best for you. Remember that there is no right or wrong answer.
- After you answer the quiz, find your praying personality by using the Assessment Key.
- If you prefer, you can also take the Praying Personalities Quiz online, using this QR code:

1. I see God as
    a. A peacemaker
    b. A friend
    c. A planner or guide
    d. A decision-maker

2. I pray when
    a. I see a problem
    b. I am sad
    c. I need a friend's encouragement
    d. Life is chaotic

3. My prayers
    a. Resemble conversations
    b. Consist of problems that need answers
    c. Ask God to give me peace
    d. Are reflections of my mood

4. When someone is speaking,
    a. I think of how to solve their problem
    b. I think about what they're saying
    c. I listen and empathize
    d. I think about sharing my story

5. The Bible
    a. Helps me know I am not alone in my prayers
    b. Has characters and stories that inspire my prayers
    c. Helps me form authoritative prayers
    d. Is a good place to go when I do not know how to pray

6. Questions are
   a. Never part of my prayers
   b. Rarely part of my prayers
   c. Sometimes part of my prayers
   d. Often part of my prayers

7. When God doesn't answer my prayers the way I want,
   a. I get confused
   b. I get sad
   c. I feel hurt
   d. I get frustrated or impatient

8. God speaks
   a. Through his Word
   b. Through my friends
   c. In my quiet space
   d. At the last minute

9. My prayer time is typically
   a. Part of my daily routine
   b. Informal but regular
   c. On the go, whenever
   d. Short and to the point

10. When crisis hits,
    a. I wait to see how God takes care of things
    b. I go to my quiet spot and pray
    c. I call my family and friends for prayer
    d. I immediately send prayer requests to prayer groups

11. When I am praying with other people,
    a. I am reluctant to express my needs
    b. I like having their prayerful company
    c. I am purposeful, focused, and succinct
    d. I am a good listener and pray silently

12. I am most comfortable praying
    a. With my family
    b. In my favorite quiet place
    c. When it's convenient
    d. With my Bible at the ready

13. When I hear of a prayer need,
    a. I write down the prayer request, date it, and wait for the answer
    b. I think about that person and pray faithfully
    c. I pray right then
    d. I call the person and pray for her or him

14. My personal prayers for myself
    a. Tend to be big and bold
    b. Are infrequent
    c. Are about friends and family
    d. Ask for help a lot

15. Meditation is
    a. Not part of my prayer routine
    b. Something that lifts my spirits
    c. Something I might do on a prayerwalk
    d. A practice I do once in a while

16. When I hear of positive answers to prayer,
    a. I send a note expressing my love
    b. I call that person to celebrate
    c. I thank God quietly
    d. I am glad I was part of that prayer network

## Assessment Key

- Circle the letter of your answer for each question in the table that follows.
- Total the number of each letter and put that number in the "Total" boxes on the last line.
- Your primary praying personality will have the highest number, but you may find there's also a fairly high number of another praying personality, because we are often combinations of two personalities. As you read the last chapter, you may have found that prayer ideas from more than one praying personality section made sense to you.
- Enjoy experimenting with different praying styles . . . and remember: the quiz is not a science, just a helpful tool for guiding you.

APPENDIX

| | Problem Solver | Friend of God | Organized Pray-er | Peace Seeker |
|---|---|---|---|---|
| 1 | d | b | c | a |
| 2 | a | c | b | d |
| 3 | b | a | d | c |
| 4 | a | d | c | b |
| 5 | c | b | a | d |
| 6 | b | a | d | c |
| 7 | d | c | b | a |
| 8 | a | b | c | d |
| 9 | b | c | a | d |
| 10 | d | c | b | a |
| 11 | c | b | a | d |
| 12 | d | a | b | c |
| 13 | c | d | a | b |
| 14 | a | c | d | b |
| 15 | c | a | b | d |
| 16 | d | b | a | c |
| Total | | | | |
| | Problem Solver | Friend of God | Organized Pray-er | Peace Seeker |

# Notes

### Chapter 1: Debunking Expectations
1. Linda Gilden and Linda Goldfarb, *LINKED: Quick Guide to Personalities* (Friendswood, TX: Bold Vision Books, 2018).
2. Herbert Lockyer, *All the Prayers of the Bible* (Grand Rapids: Zondervan, 1959).

### Chapter 3: Emotive Pray-ers
1. Pam Farrel, Jean E. Jones, and Karla Dornacher, *Discovering Hope in the Psalms* (Eugene, OR: Harvest House, 2017), 17, 39, 41, 64, 91, 136, 139, 190.
2. Herbert Lockyer, *All the Prayers of the Bible* (Grand Rapids: Zondervan, 1959), 136.

### Chapter 4: Devotional Pray-ers
1. The referenced Elisha stories are in the following Scriptures: 2 Kings 4:1–7 (widow's oil), 2 Kings 4:8–17 (Shunammite woman bears a son), 2 Kings 4:18–37 (Shunammite woman's son is restored to life), and 2 Kings 5:1–15 (Naaman's healing from leprosy).
2. Mark Batterson, *Draw the Circle: The 40 Day Prayer Challenge* (Grand Rapids: Zondervan, 2012), 43.

## Chapter 5: Physical Pray-ers

1. Herbert Lockyer, *All the Prayers of the Bible* (Grand Rapids: Zondervan, 1959), 29.
2. Elmer L. Towns, *Fasting for Spiritual Breakthrough: A Guide to Nine Biblical Fasts* (Ventura, CA: Regal Books, 1996), 15.
3. Note: In the same story, Mark in his Gospel records Jesus saying, "This kind can come out only by prayer" (9:29).
4. Towns, *Fasting*, 5–6.

## Chapter 6: Jesus, the Model for Prayer

1. Richard J. Foster, *Prayer: Finding the Heart's True Home* (San Francisco: HarperSanFrancisco, 1992), 185.
2. Justin Taylor, "C. S. Lewis on the Theology and Practice of Worship," The Gospel Coalition, October 20, 2015, https://www.the gospelcoalition.org/blogs/justin-taylor/c-s-lewis-on-the-theology -and-practice-of-worship/.
3. W. E. Vine, *Expository Dictionary of New Testament Words*, vol. 2 (Old Tappan, NJ: Revell, 1966), 152.
4. Janet Holm McHenry, *The Complete Guide to the Prayers of Jesus: What Jesus Prayed and How It Will Change Your Life Today* (Minneapolis: Bethany House, 2018), 120.
5. Jackie Green and Lauren Green McAfee, "The Praying Example of Susanna Wesley," Faith Gateway, accessed January 2, 2023, https://faithgateway.com/blogs/christian-books/praying-example -susanna-wesley.

## Chapter 7: Paul, the On-the-Run Intercessor

1. Brother Lawrence, *The Practice of the Presence of God* (North Brunswick, NJ: Bridge-Logos Publishers, 1999), 5.
2. Janet Holm McHenry, *PrayerStreaming: Staying in Touch with God All Day Long* (Colorado Springs: WaterBrook, 2005).

3. D. A. Carson, *Praying with Paul: A Call to Spiritual Reformation* (Grand Rapids: Baker Academic, 2014), 48.

4. Carson, *Praying with Paul*, 48.

5. Carson, *Praying with Paul*, 55.

### Chapter 9 : The Modern Personalities

1. While the test the students took was not identified at the time, it was Gary Smalley who created this animal personality assessment. More information is here: Gary Smalley, "Personality Test," The Smalley Institute, accessed July 25, 2022, https://www.accounseling.org/wp-content/uploads/2018/10/Personality-Test-Smalley.pdf. Also available in Chapter 10, "Understanding Personality Types: A Key to Lovability," *Making Love Last Forever* (Nashville: Thomas Nelson, 1997).

2. Simon Sinek, "How to Leverage Being an Introvert," YouTube, November 25, 2020, https://www.youtube.com/watch?v=ozSjZ6iRKSA.

3. Isabel Briggs Myers with Peter B. Myers, *Gifts Differing: Understanding Personality Type* (Mountain View, CA: Consulting Psychologists Press, 1995), xi–xv.

4. "Myers & Briggs' 16 Personality Types," Truity, accessed February 6, 2023, https://www.truity.com/page/16-personality-types-myers-briggs.

5. "Kiersey Temperament Sorter," City Vision University, accessed August 25, 2022, https://library.cityvision.edu/keirsey-temperament-sorter#:~:text=Historical%20development,related%20to%20the%20four%20temperaments.

6. "Core Theory: Our Framework," 16 Personalities, 2022, https://www.16personalities.com/articles/our-theory#intro.

7. "Donald O. Clifton," Wikipedia, accessed July 10, 2022, https://en.wikipedia.org/wiki/Donald_O._Clifton.

8. "What Are the Big 5 Personality Traits?," Thomas International, November 1, 2022, https://www.thomas.co/resources/type/hr-gui des/what-are-big-5-personality-traits#:~:text=The%20five%20 broad%20personality%20traits,openness%2C%20conscientious ness%2C%20and%20neuroticism.

## Chapter 10: The Enneagram

1. "Fourth Way," Wikipedia, accessed March 16, 2022, https:// en.wikipedia.org/wiki/Fourth_Way.
2. Joe Carter, "The FAQs: What Christians Should Know about the Enneagram," The Gospel Coalition, August 8, 2018, https:// www.thegospelcoalition.org/article/the-faqs-what-christians -should-know-about-the-enneagram/.
3. Marilyn Jansen, *Inspired by Prayer: A Creative Prayer Journal* (New York: Ellie Claire/Hachette, 2019).

## Chapter 11: Generational Personalities

1. Jeffrey M. Jones, "U.S. Church Membership Falls Below Ma- jority for First Time," Gallup, March 29, 2021, https://news .gallup.com/poll/341963/church-membership-falls-below-ma jority-first-time.aspx#:~:text=U.S.%20church%20member ship%20was%2073,2010%20and%2047%25%20in%202020.
2. Randall Balmer, "Billy Graham: American Evangelist," Britan- nica, accessed July 3, 2022, https://www.britannica.com/biogra phy/Billy-Graham.
3. Jeffrey M. Jones, "U.S. Church Membership."
4. Jessica Sager, "What Generation Am I?," Parade, June 29, 2022, https://parade.com/1113130/jessicasager/generation-names-and -years/.
5. "Generation Jones," The Jones Group, accessed August 8, 2022, https://www.generationjones.com/?page_id=6.

6. "CBA," Wikipedia, accessed January 28, 2023, https://en.wikipedia.org/wiki/CBA_(Christian_trade_association).

7. Jessica Sager, "What Generation Am I?"

8. Carol Howard Merritt, "Why Doesn't Anyone Care about Generation X?," The Christian Century, August 14, 2013, https://www.christiancentury.org/blogs/archive/2013-08/why-doesn-t-anyone-care-about-generation-x.

9. Marney A. White, "The History of ADHD: A Timeline," Healthline, October 28, 2021, https://www.healthline.com/health/adhd/history#1902.

10. "The Whys and Hows of Generation Research," Pew Research, September 3, 2015, https://www.pewresearch.org/politics/2015/09/03/the-whys-and-hows-of-generations-research/#key-differences-between-the-generations.

11. Jessica Sager, "What Generation Am I?"

12. Hillary Hoffower and Allana Akhtar, "Lonely, Burned Out, and Depressed: The State of Millenials' Mental Health in 2020," Business Insider, October 10, 2020, https://www.businessinsider.com/millennials-mental-health-burnout-lonely-depressed-money-stress#depression-is-on-the-rise-among-millennials-2.

13. Jessica Sager, "What Generation Am I?"

14. Daniel A. Cox, "Generation Z and the Future of Faith in America," Survey Center on American Life, March 25, 2022, https://www.americansurveycenter.org/research/generation-z-future-of-faith.

### Chapter 13: Ministry Gifts

1. John Piper, "Spiritual Gifts," Desiring God, March 15, 1981, https://www.desiringgod.org/messages/spiritual-gifts.

2. The NIV Study Bible, Kenneth Barker, ed. (Grand Rapids: Zondervan, 1985), notes, 1750.

3. The NIV Study Bible, notes, 1795.

4. Richard Foster, *Prayer: Finding the Heart's True Home* (New York: HarperSanFrancisco, 1992), 246.

5. Debbie Kitterman, *The Gift of Prophetic Encouragement: Hearing the Words of God for Others* (Minneapolis: Chosen Books, 2018), 67–68.

6. *The NIV Study Bible*, notes, 1497–1498.

7. W. E. Vine, *Expository Dictionary of New Testament Words*, vol. 1 (Old Tappan, NJ: Revell, 1966), 63.

8. D. Guthrie et al., eds., *The New Bible Commentary*, rev. ed. (Grand Rapids: Eerdmans, 1970), 116.

9. W. E. Vine, *Expository Dictionary of New Testament Words*, vol. 2 (Old Tappan, NJ: Revell, 1966), 44.

10. *The NIV Study Bible*, notes, 1795.

11. Mandy Smith et al., "Pastor, How Do You Pray for Your Church?," ChristianityToday.com, accessed September 1, 2022, https://www.christianitytoday.com/pastors/2017/april-web-ex clusives/pastor-how-do-you-pray-for-your-church.html.

12. Stephen Altrogge, "So Busy That I MUST Pray," Church Leaders, accessed June 19, 2023, https://churchleaders.com/worship /worship-blogs/160046-stephen_altrogge_so_busy_that_i _must_pray.html.

13. "A Quick List of Biblical Spiritual Gifts: Which Gifts Exist and What They Mean," Tyndale, *Unfolding Faith Blog*, 2018, https:// www.tyndale.com/sites/unfoldingfaithblog/2019/10/01/a-quick -list-of-biblical-spiritual-gifts-which-gifts-exist-and-what-they -mean/.

14. W. E. Vine, *Expository Dictionary*, vol. 2, 213.

## Chapter 14: Manifestation Gifts

1. *The NIV Study Bible*, Kenneth Barker, ed. (Grand Rapids: Zondervan, 1985), notes, 1750.

2. W. E. Vine, *Expository Dictionary of New Testament Words*, vol. 2 (Old Tappan, NJ: Revell, 1966), 301.

3. W. E. Vine, *Expository Dictionary*, vol. 2, 71.

4. "A Quick List of Biblical Spiritual Gifts: Which Gifts Exist and What They Mean," Tyndale, *Unfolding Faith Blog*, 2018, https://www.tyndale.com/sites/unfoldingfaithblog/2019/10/01/a-quick-list-of-biblical-spiritual-gifts-which-gifts-exist-and-what-they-mean/.

5. George Müller, *Release the Power of Prayer* (New Kensington, PA: Whitaker House, 1999), 6–7.

6. George Müller, *Answers to Prayer*, ed. A. E. C. Brooks (Chicago: Moody Press, 1984), 12–13.

7. Russell Moore, "The Gift of Healing: Is It Still for Today?," Christianity.com, October 4, 2011, https://www.christianity.com/jesus/following-jesus/fruit-of-the-spirit/is-the-gift-of-healing-for-today.html.

8. *The NIV Study Bible*, notes, 1750.

9. W. E. Vine, *Expository Dictionary of New Testament Words*, vol. 3 (Old Tappan, NJ: Revell, 1966), 75.

10. *The NIV Study Bible*, notes, 1724.

11. W. E. Vine, *Expository Dictionary of New Testament Words*, vol. 1 (Old Tappan, NJ: Revell, 1966), 315, 281.

12. *The NIV Study Bible*, notes, 1750.

### Chapter 15: Motivational Gifts

1. W. E. Vine, *Expository Dictionary of New Testament Words*, vol. 3 (Old Tappan, NJ: Revell Company, 1966), 58.

2. W. E. Vine, *Expository Dictionary of New Testament Words*, vol. 2 (Old Tappan, NJ: Revell, 1966), 26.

3. *The NIV Study Bible*, Kenneth Barker, ed. (Grand Rapids: Zondervan, 1985), notes, 1725.

4. "Kybernesis," Blue Letter Bible, accessed September 30, 2022, https://www.blueletterbible.org/lexicon/g2941/nkjv/tr/0-1/.
5. Richard J. Foster, *Prayer: Finding the Heart's True Home* (New York: HarperCollins, 1992), vii.
6. W. E. Vine, *Expository Dictionary*, vol. 3, 61.

### Chapter 16: Finding Your Praying Style

1. Richard Baxter, *The Saints' Everlasting Rest*, ed. Tim Cooper, ed. (Wheaton, IL: Crossway, 2022), 114. Note: This is an updated and abridged version of the original 1650 version.